BUILDINGS MATTER

SECOND EDITION

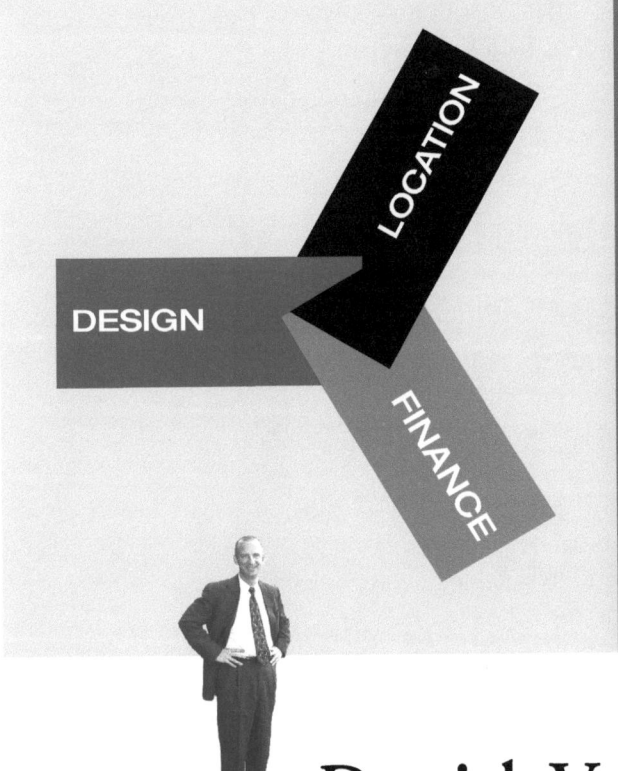

Why Buildings Can Make or Break Your Business

Derrick Van Mell

Tranton Press Books

Cover designed by Broadbent & Williams
Interior layout by Flying Pig Productions
Author photographs by John Devereux

ISBN 0-9770914-1-4

Tranton Press Books
P.O. Box 6554
Madison, WI 53716

Copyright © 2010 Derrick Van Mell

All rights reserved, including the right of reproduction in whole or in part in any form.

To Susan, Trina, and Clayton.
You make our house a home.

TABLE OF CONTENTS

Introduction 1

Leadership
   1 ▪ A Privilege of Leadership 3
   2 ▪ The Project Plan and Its Business Case 7

Logic: Location, Finance, Design
   3 ▪ Location: The Science and Art of Place 17
   4 ▪ Finance: Easy Analysis vs. Hard Decisions 47
   5 ▪ Design: Practical and Psychological Functions 57

Implementation
   6 ▪ Executive Team and Tasks 105
   7 ▪ Grand Opening 113

Acknowledgments 115
Bibliography 117
Image Credits 119
About the Author 121

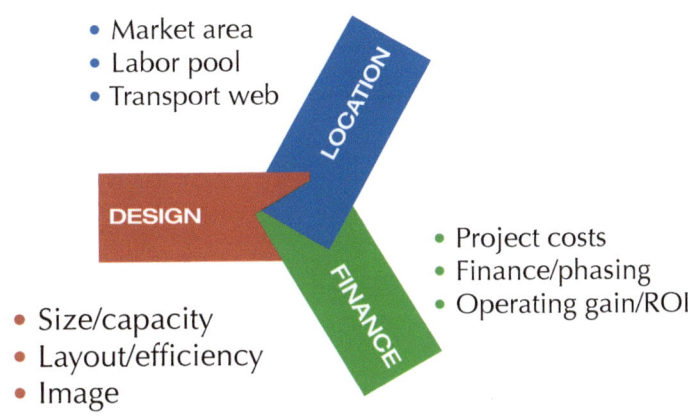

Make no little plans; they have no magic to stir men's blood and probably will themselves not be realized. Make big plans; aim high in hope and work, remembering that a noble, logical diagram once recorded will not die.

Daniel Burnham

Introduction

Building is a privilege a leader cannot escape. This book is for the CEOs, deans, directors, and statesmen who must inspire their organizations and equip them for success. This book answers key questions about buildings, such as:

- Should we renovate or build new?
- Where should our building be?
- How should we pay for it?
- How do I establish a budget?
- Should our building fit in or stand out?
- How do I hire and guide my architect?
- How should I budget my time?
- How do I *think* about all these decisions?"

Chapter 1 explores the leadership opportunities in building a building: it looks beyond the risks and complexities to the greater goals and greater good.

Chapter 2 defines the facility plan and its business case, the planner's critical first step.

Chapter 3 provides an illustrated framework for location analysis using maps from many industries.

Chapter 4 is a concise, spreadsheet-free discussion of the core financial issues and analyses, including lease vs. own.

Chapter 5 outlines the practical and psychological functions of design and proves those ideas in famous buildings and familiar industries.

Chapter 6 tells how to select and work with an architect and builder through grand opening.

Decisions about buildings take enormous courage, so I want to acknowledge the many brave leaders with whom I have worked over the past twenty years. They have challenged and improved my thinking from the executive's point of view, which is why this second edition includes new sections on location and financial analysis.

1 · A Privilege of Leadership

Power Used Wisely

The Pentagon broke ground on September 11, 1941 and was completed in only 16 months. At 6.6 million square feet, it was not just an incredible engineering feat: President Roosevelt had given the United States a powerful practical and psychological advantage in winning the war.

Winston Churchill clearly stated the lasting opportunity of architecture: "We shape our buildings; thereafter, our buildings shape us." Through their buildings, the leader proclaims his or her vision, shows resolve, and shapes the corporate culture for decades. To build wisely is to lead well.

Figure 1.1 The Pentagon

During the Blitz, Churchill hastily built a maze of underground war rooms in the heart of London. It promoted leadership through its brave location, its make-do-ness, and its cramped, intense spaces. Every inch was given to winning the war. (It is a museum today.) In contrast, Hitler and his architect, Albert Speer, created a plan of buildings for Berlin that were oppressive and monumental (figure 1.2).

4 BUILDINGS MATTER

Der Führer vor dem Modell des gigantischen Kongreßbaues

Figure 1.2 Hitler and building model, 1937

A different example of architecture's role in leadership sits near Detroit. In 1991, Lee Iacocca opened the Chrysler Technology Center (CTC), a 2.6 million square foot, $1 billion consolidation of Chrysler's new car development departments. The CTC helped Chrysler accelerate bringing new cars to market and fend off foreign competitors. The practical effects were clear and the message was clear, too: We know where we're going, and we've got the ideas and guts to get there.

Successful buildings are memorable and most failures quickly forgotten: buildings so poorly planned that their owners are forced to change them, ignore them, and finally, leave them.

Risks and Opportunities

There are nine common risks for the leader in any building project:

1. Overspending, which drains cash, drags down corporate return on assets, and weakens credit strength
2. Underspending and finding oneself short of the capacity needed to fulfill one's goals
3. Locating in the wrong market area, limiting customer access and visibility, reducing sales, and creating a competitive vulnerability
4. Locating in the wrong labor pool, forever catching up on turnover, productivity, and consistently higher cost of goods or services
5. Building permanent inefficiencies, through poor layout and workflow or by losing economies of scale among many buildings
6. Board dissension from a poorly managed decision-making process. A 51% approval is riskier than a 49% loss with an opportunity for revision
7. Community resentment from unfortunate publicity or failing to bring the expected jobs and local sales
8. Lack of flexibility that is either costly or fatal
9. Wasting time and energy

The purpose of this book is to guide the readers around these obstacles in decisions about buildings, and then to point them toward confident decisions and success for their organizations and themselves. A good planner will challenge the leader to think about the past, present, and future in new ways.

Vision and Courage

A building is a billboard of the leader's vision. A well-designed building declares the leader's commitment to high quality products or services, thoughtful customer relations, caring management, and the community's health. It reminds everyone daily of his or her purpose and importance.

A leader takes risks for both fortune and honor. Being the first to build in a new market is one way to win customer attention and respect. Building is always bold, and customers, staff, board members, and bankers want the leader to prove his or her courage and confidence. The success or failure of a building is easy to see.

Culture and Morale

A leader molds the organization's culture, be it formal or informal, hierarchical or consensual, bold or quiet, ambitious or steady. A building, by its location, shape, landscaping, colors, lighting, furniture, and art, constantly signals the organization's values. A building is the silent backdrop everywhere people meet, work, learn, eat, and socialize. Ernest Dimnet said, "Architecture, of all the arts, acts most slowly, yet most surely on the soul." Almost everyone is keenly attuned to his or her surroundings. The leader's indifference to the building will be felt every day as indifference to the employees.

The leader's own space interests everyone and special care should be given to the message it sends. While Hitler's office (figure 1.3) was designed to intimidate, it is not wrong to build a quiet symbol of authority, style, and stability. In Chapter 5, we see Franklin D. Roosevelt at his desk in the Oval Office.

Providing Capacity for Success

Leadership takes much more than symbols of vision and culture. A building is a hard-working piece of equipment for crafting high quality goods and services. Everyone every day depends on their building so they can work well on their individual tasks and work well as a team. A good building is a good tool: it helps everyone who uses it do a better, more satisfying job.

Figure 1.3 Hitler's office, Nazi postcard

2 · THE PROJECT PLAN AND ITS BUSINESS CASE

Architecture is not just about fulfilling space needs or drawing an attractive building. A successful project plan encompasses all the business requirements of the project: its location and financial aspects and its appropriateness to the organization's overall business plan. As the pace of change accelerates, so does the need for careful thinking about what a building will mean the year it is completed and for decades to come.

The Big Questions

A common and costly mistake is to build a building for one reason alone, such as to acquire more space or enter a geographic market or consolidate operations. An early analysis of needs must be undertaken. Certain tough questions must be answered before the design process starts:

- ❑ What kind of site is appropriate?
- ❑ What effects must the building have on the customers and staff?
- ❑ Is this huge investment necessary?
- ❑ Should we renovate or build new?
- ❑ How much will the project cost?
- ❑ Where should it be located?
- ❑ What size should the first phase of construction be?
- ❑ To what size should the building be able to grow?
- ❑ What are the big risks of undertaking this project?
- ❑ What are the risks of *not* undertaking this project?
- ❑ How must the building boost efficiency?

- How will we pay for it?
- How can this big change be managed?
- Who on the board of directors will support it, and why?
- Who on the board will *not* support it, and why not?
- Who will make the decisions?
- Who will manage the project?
- When must the project start and end?
- When are all the decisions needed from the leader?

The leader must establish a project planning team to answer these questions. While the architect or a specialty consultant can lead this effort, the team should include senior managers and at least a representative of the staff and one of the directors. A stark truth of building is that the presentation of the plan is often distilled into a 15-minute presentation to the board. As was said in Chapter 1, the leader cannot escape the responsibility of his or her decision; it is a career turning point.

Core Logic

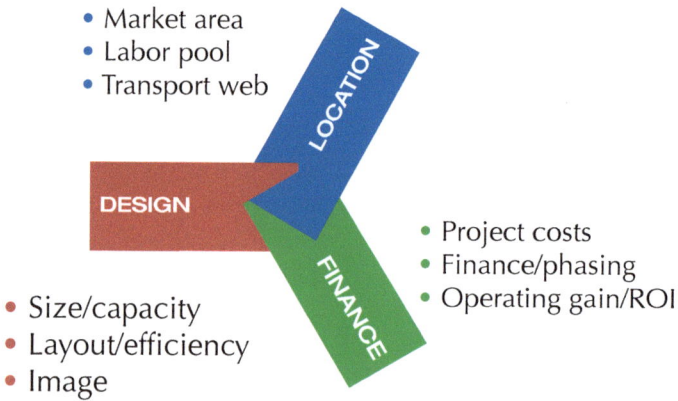

Figure 2.1 Project planning logic

Every project plan integrates issues and analyses of location, design, and finance (figure 2.1). Location concerns the forces of the marketplace, labor pool, community, and transportation. In the project plan, the space use analysis—provided by the architect—is concerned with the general parameters of size, workflow, and infrastructure. The finance concerns are cost, timing, affordability, financing, liquidity, and ultimately, return. These analyses are needed to answer the big questions listed earlier.

Project planning is an emerging field and its associated terms are often confusing. Architects, builders, consultants, and bankers might use the terms *feasibility study, master plan* and *strategic facility plan* interchangeably, as these all answer the basic question: What projects must we undertake to have the buildings that support our long-term business plan? But there area differences: a *master plan* is based on assumptions provided by the managers, while a true project plan or a *strategic facility plan* includes general business analyses (such as a market assessment, competitor analysis, or workflow study) to support or update those assumptions.

The Business Case and its Effects on the P&L

The key financial question is, What will our financial statements look like if we choose plan A or plan B? Here is yet another challenge for the project planners: estimating how a well-designed and well-located building changes the key line items on the income statement or P&L: revenue, payroll, and other major direct and indirect costs. The ROI worksheet (figure 2.2) is a tool for answering these questions.

Every leader knows to test a project concept before submitting it for board approval. That concept becomes the object of a business case, which has three ingredients: a complete description of the concept (at just the right level of detail), a clear statement why the project supports the organization's mission, and proof that the concept yields the best return of capital, time, and risk. It is not trivial to make the business case concise and enthusiastic.

FINANCIAL PERFORMANCE IMPROVEMENTS		
REVENUE	Market share	_____ %
Rationale: Visibility, sales management, customer access	Product revenue	_____
	Service revenue	_____
		$100
COST OF GOODS SOLD	Direct labor	_____
Rationale: Workflow, morale, supplier access, shipping costs, utilities	OT labor	_____
	Raw materials	_____
	Shipping	_____
	Inventory costs	_____
		$70
OVERHEAD	Supervisory labor	_____
Rationale: Centralization, facility financing, standardization	Facilities	_____
	Interest expense	_____
	Depreciation	_____
	Taxes	_____
		$10
PROFIT (LOSS) / SF		$20

Figure 2.2 ROI worksheet

Objectives Based on Business Goals

Some Typical Objectives

Many executives set project objectives that are too simple and then find their projects adrift. To say only, "I know what I want: an efficient, attractive building in a good location that doesn't cost too much" is to invite disaster. These tough-sounding objectives are indisputable, but meaningless. The leader must instead consider how each business goal for marketing, operations, staffing, and corporate finance relates to the building's location, design, and financial performance—and to the P&L. The result is often 12–18 specific and measurable objectives, which can be framed on a one-page scorecard (figure 2.3).

MATCH TO OBJECTIVES	WEIGHT	CURRENT		A		B	
		\multicolumn{6}{c}{SCORE / WEIGHTED SCORE}					
1 Achieve high visibility within community	3	2	6	4	12	5	15
2 Ensure easy access for customers and staff	5	3	15	4	20	5	25
3 Enhance facility tour from approach through exit	3	2	6	4	12	4	12
4 Size plant for 5-year projections	5	2	10	5	25	4	20
5 Accommodate new inventory and material management	4	2	8	5	20	4	16
6 Provide for added office staff per business plan	4	3	12	5	20	4	16
7 Be able to expand on site by 250% over 10 years	4	1	4	5	20	3	12
8 Provide a safe and healthy work environment	5	3	15	5	25	3	15
9 Ensure easy workflows in all departments	5	1	5	5	25	5	25
10 Enhance on-site access by suppliers	3	2	6	4	12	3	9
11 Locate within overlap of best labor pools	5	1	5	5	25	4	20
12 Improve communications among all groups	5	2	10	5	25	4	20
13 Protect resale value	4	3	12	4	16	5	20
14 Protect access to capital	4	3	12	4	16	5	20
BENEFITS			**126**		**273**		**245**
COSTS							
PROJECT TOTAL ($M)					**$16.8**		**$14.8**
ADDED CASH FLOW ($M)					**$2.5**		**$2.3**
OCCUPANCY COSTS ($K)					**$713**		**$675**

Figure 2.3 Project scorecard

For example, a common revenue goal is to increase market share, which would shape several facility objectives: one supporting location objective might be to either move to or add a building in a market area, or to renovate one's current location. The same market share goal can shape a space use objective, such as to expand capacity significantly.

Another common business goal is to reduce labor costs by increasing worker productivity. This goal may drive a location objective to relocate to a better labor pool. It may also define a space use objective to create a technology-dependent layout that allows work to be produced with less human labor.

Architecture is not just about creating pretty buildings; it is about creating a practical tool of leadership. This is why creating a complete and compelling statement of objectives is the first vital step in winning board approval *and* of good design. The next steps include developing the best information and solutions, and distilling the recommendation into a compelling plan. As frontiersman Daniel Boone said, "Be sure that you're right—then go ahead."

Location is the Context of Architecture

The choice of location is as important to the facility plan as are choices about space use and finance. The location does as much to fulfill the objectives as the structure itself. How would one use and feel about their office, shop, or church if it were in the wrong place? The architect might not be able to address these issues, but should know someone who can, such as a project planner, market analyst, or demographer. See Chapter 3 for more about location analysis.

Sophisticated mapping can depict the intricate forces of the market, labor pool, and transportation web at levels useful to managers and directors. Aerial photographs are easily found on the Internet; they give another rich perspective on one's prospective neighborhood.

The map in figure 2.4 is part of a location analysis for the Goodman Community Center in Madison, Wisconsin. It shows demographics, neighborhood borders, bus routes, pedestrian walking times, and the location of participants and donors. The small pie

Figure 2.4 Atwood Community Center map

charts show the degree of home ownership in each neighborhood. In addition to guiding the location decision, this powerful picture speaks to the future of the Center's programs, the kind of new participants to expect, and therefore, the corporate image it wants to portray to its users. Because the Center receives government funding, the map helped prove its eligibility for certain kinds of capital and operational financing.

Location analysis and site selection differ. Location analysis deals with geography in general sense; in Chapter 5 we talk specifically about the site itself.

Market Place, Labor Pool, and Transportation Web

A coffee shop's design should be defined by its marketplace. The projected number of customers will determine the shop's size, and market research about customer tastes will frame decisions about the look of the storefront and interior.

A study of one's labor pools will yield similar insights. Knowing what kind of people will work in a building will inform the project's feasibility and character. Long commutes strain a labor pool; the ideal is a location neatly woven into a neighborhood rich with housing, schools, healthcare, and shops: people want to *belong* to a place. Lands' End succeeds in Dodgeville, Wisconsin because Gary Comer, the founder and first CEO, foresaw that access to good labor would be a competitive advantage.

Analyzing the project's transportation web is vital, too. Knowing how customers, staff, and suppliers will get to and from the building will guide choices about location, parking, the number of docks, storage spaces, and so on. The *frequency* of these visits is another factor in the size of the site and building.

The Psychology of Location

The location affects the psychological success of the building. The leader must consider proximity to nature, the need for prestige and status, and family and community participation. A costly location on Wall Street might suit investment bankers, but a community center will choose another type of location.

Space Use Planning

The Program

The analysis of space use (what architects call the *program*) establishes the spaces needed, but not how they look. The program sets forth how much space is to be built in each project phase, the basic arrangement to allow smooth workflow, and infrastructure needs, such as ceiling heights, column spacing, and mechanical systems.

The Project Plan and Its Business Case 13

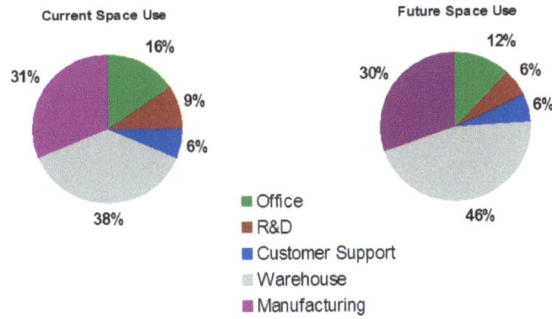

Figure 2.5 Space use allocation

The program is compiled with spreadsheets listing each room's size and is subtotaled by department and floor. These subtotals can then be charted and graphed to compare to the past and to industry averages (figure 2.5).

Programming forces tough decisions: the long-term projection of size depends on the leader's projections of the numbers of employees and customers, the volume of work, and how that work will be done. A building offers no ambiguity behind which to hide: it cannot be built for 100 *and* for 200 people. While flexibility is possible, with excess land, excess space, and modularity, the program forces decisions that show the leader's confidence in the future.

The Adjacency Analysis and Block Plan

A *workflow diagram,* or *adjacency analysis,* charts how people connect to do their work, whether they are assembling things or working with ideas. New technologies and management theories can radically realign how people and departments interact.

The last space use analysis in the project plan is the *block plan,* a simple drawing (often color-coded, figure 2.6) that plots the relative size and arrangement of spaces. The block plan is the starting point for the design, discussed in Chapter 5.

Figure 2.6 Block plan

Financial Analysis

Project Budget and Annual Expenses

The program and the block plan allow a builder or estimator to create the project budget. A budget includes the cost of the building and land, as well as closing costs for the site, design of the building, and financing the project. The costs of fixtures, furniture, equipment, and relocation must also be included in the total.

Annual expenses need to be estimated, too. Interest or rent is usually the largest items of facility expense; other expenses are utilities, maintenance, and property taxes. Depreciation, amortization, and principal contributions might be shown separately. The leader should also set aside funds for long-term maintenance, such as reroofing, unexpected repairs, and so on. Chapter 4 deals with financial issues in depth.

Financing and Timing

The next questions concern financing: sources of funds, degree of leverage, interest rate risk strategies, covenants, and so forth. Creative financing varies among industries, and the availability, costs, and risks of financing types directly affect the project's timing, size, and market value.

One big question is, How large should the first phase of construction be? Many financial factors shape the phasing decision: affordability, economies of scale, market risk, financial risks (inflation, rates, and availability), and the cost of business disruption. This, too, is a tough decision that must be resolved in the project plan—not while designing.

Return on Investment

The ROI analysis (figure 2.2) defines one basic measure of financial success. Other financial measures compare facility alternatives: debt coverage ratio, administrative expense ratio, days' cash on hand, inventory turns, and average revenue or direct costs per unit, among others. Not-for-profit institutions use similar ratios. Qualitative benefits are ranked at the end of this process.

A building's effects on financial performance are strong, and so a defensible pro forma is necessary for good decisions, board approval, and for loan applications or bond underwriting. Discounted cash flow analyses (Net Present Value, Internal Rate of Return) can cloak the tough questions about how a well-located and well-designed building will change basic financial performance. Many projects stall or stumble because the pro forma was either too conservative or not conservative enough—or because too much attention was given to complex schemes and spreadsheets.

Making a Brave Decision

Every leader has a personal style of decision making: some are intuitive, others analytical. The leader must decide at the outset who participates, what level of analysis is needed, and how to brief the board and staff on progress. It is essential to genuinely address each audience's concerns. A well-supported decision is a powerful basis for all the negotiations for services and financing that lie ahead.

Creative Leap

At some point, one must take the creative leap to blend all the information about location, design, and financing into alternative concepts that meet the objectives. Basic alternatives are the Ideal, Next Best, Low Cost, and Do Nothing options, which the planning team can then distill into the single best concept.

Scoring Alternatives

In the end, a decision must be taken whether to proceed. One way to bring this complex decision into focus is to employ a scorecard using each objective as a weighted decision factor (figure 2.3); how well each alternative meets the objectives is a scientific way to rank the qualitative issues. The leader can frame the decision on one page if the scorecard also includes each alternative's costs, return, and benefits. The project plan and its business case are then ready for board approval.

One CEO described his decision making this way: "I never make a big decision until I can sit at my desk with the critical papers in front of me and feel *physically* comfortable when I imagine going ahead. If I feel a muscle twitch or tighten, I know something hasn't been resolved. But when I do decide, I feel a great sense of relief, because I know something great is going to happen."

3 · LOCATION: THE SCIENCE AND ART OF PLACE

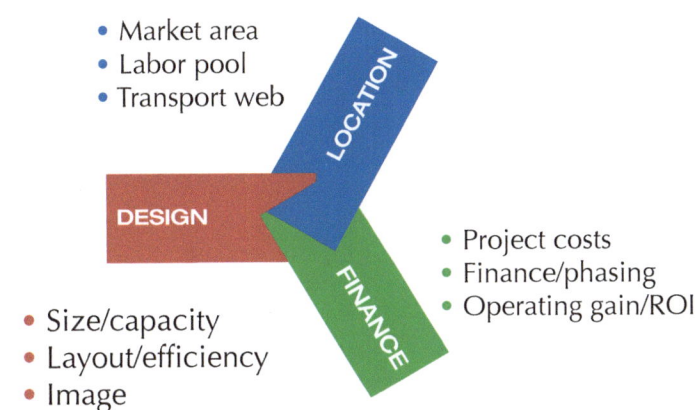

ZIP vs. Scatter

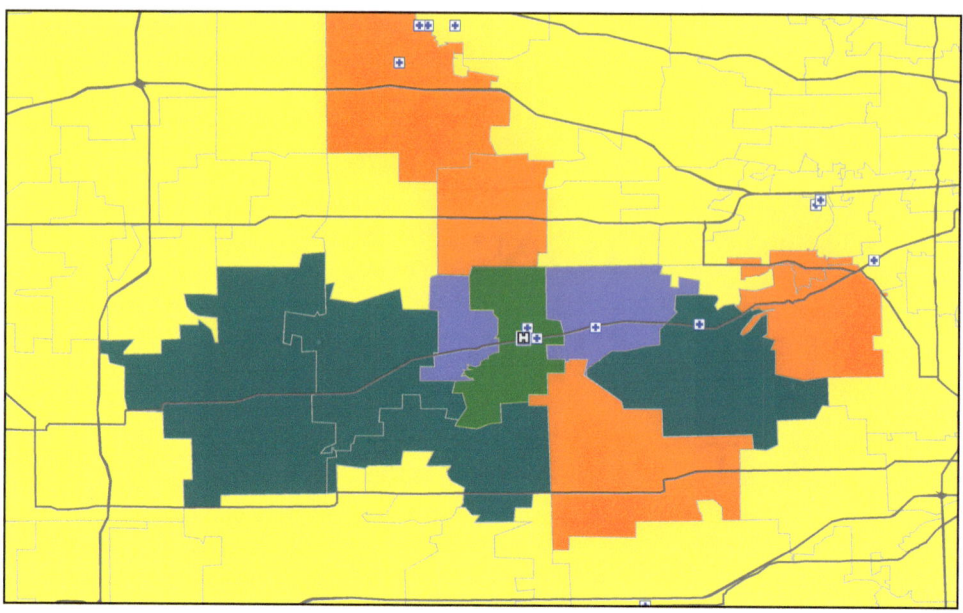

Figure 3.1 ZIP code map

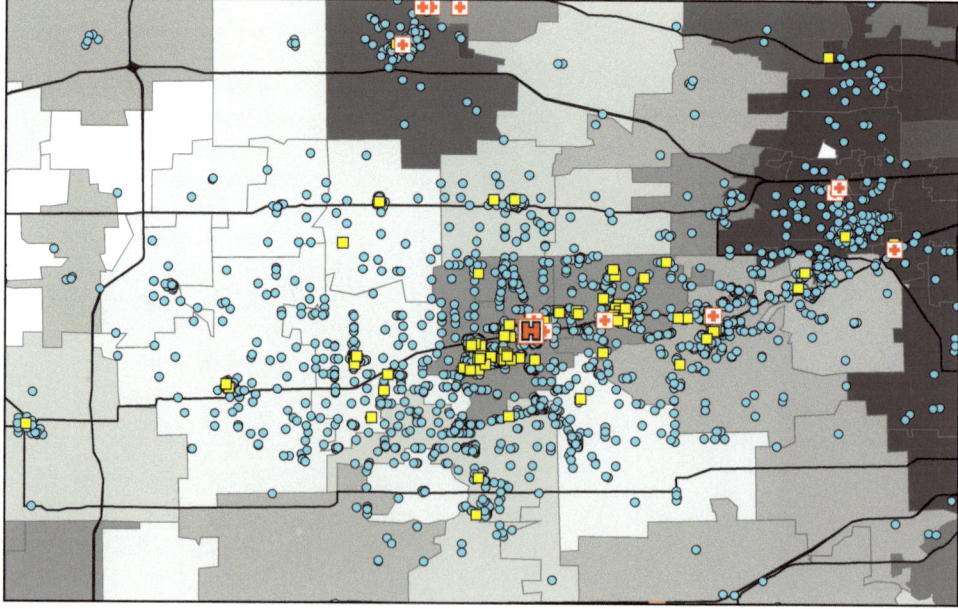

Figure 3.2 Scatter map

These two maps show why scatter maps, though a little harder to make, are so much better than ZIP codes for analyzing a market area. The map in figure 3.1 shows the density of a hospital's patients by ZIP code, what the healthcare industry calls a "patient origin study." (Remember that ZIP codes boundaries were set by the Postal Service in the 1950's and 60's for managing mail pick up and delivery—nothing to do with hospital patients.)

In contrast, the scatter map on the opposite page (figure 3.2) uses red dots to show exactly where the patients live. The heavy red lines trace around patient clusters, a much more realistic depiction of market boundary, even though it ignores some widely scatter rural patients. One can see that the market area is defined by a set of cities, town, and highway corridors. It's clear the ZIP boundaries have no bearing on how the hospital's patient relate geographically.

Why is this so important? *First,* hospital project planners must accurately project volumes of market share and therefore use—of clinic visits, inpatients, and emergency room use—in order to size their new, $100,000,000 building. To do that, they must know their total population base; the ZIP code map shows an area of 563 square miles; the scatter map boundary is 312 square miles. *Second,* the hospital needs a clear-eyed marketing plan: where to advertise, where to form physician alliances, and where to build outlying clinics. *Third,* a realistic market boundary helps planners understand how transportation and land use development will affect their market over the very long term.

Needless to say, using the wrong information would have been disastrous (as it so often is) not only for the hospital, but for the careers of the CEO and his planning team.

The Power of Place

Leaders from Alexander to Magellan knew the power of maps to learn and to plan. Winston Churchill in particular loved maps and would understand perfectly how to use them in business.

The right location will win the best position in a market area, which will in turn define the size and mix of spaces within the building. The right location will reach deeper into a labor pool, the depth and character of which will directly influence the building's image and quality. The building's location should also optimize the delivery and therefore storage of supplies and materials. Taken all together, these location factors underpin the building's return on investment. This section will show leaders how new mapping techniques and technology can help them have the right building in the right place at the right time.

Location is the context of architecture. Each location is a focal point of the leader's opportunities, costs, and risks, and the design must make the building capitalize on those opportunities. While some organizations are less location-sensitive than others, even an entirely web-based business with an international market (Amazon.com) still needs to tap big labor pools and to manage geographic distribution.

The study of location links to almost every aspect of marketing and sales, operations and logistics, staff recruitment and retention, and resource allocation. In addition to location analysis, maps can be used for:

- Marketing and distributing products and services
- Analyzing a competitor's strengths and weaknesses
- Managing sales territories
- Planning a media campaign
- Identifying underserved neighborhoods
- Recruiting a mix of staff types
- Routing materials and products from suppliers to customers

There are of course trade-offs to be made in location decisions: demographics and local transportation might make one location great for a medical office building, but perhaps the community doesn't provide a good source of staff housing. A thorough analysis of location will steer the leader through these choices.

Location: The Science and Art of Place   21

It's natural to think that location analysis is done solely with maps, but we'll see that geographic information can also be shown in a table or business graphic like a pie chart. This section will help leaders and other decision-makers take advantage of the powerful new science and art of location analysis. We will:

- Inspire leaders to take more interest in their geography
- Show how to think about location information
- Share industry-specific ideas
- Introduce the basics of good map design
- Discuss how to present maps and other location information
- Provide 10 steps to getting started on one's own analysis

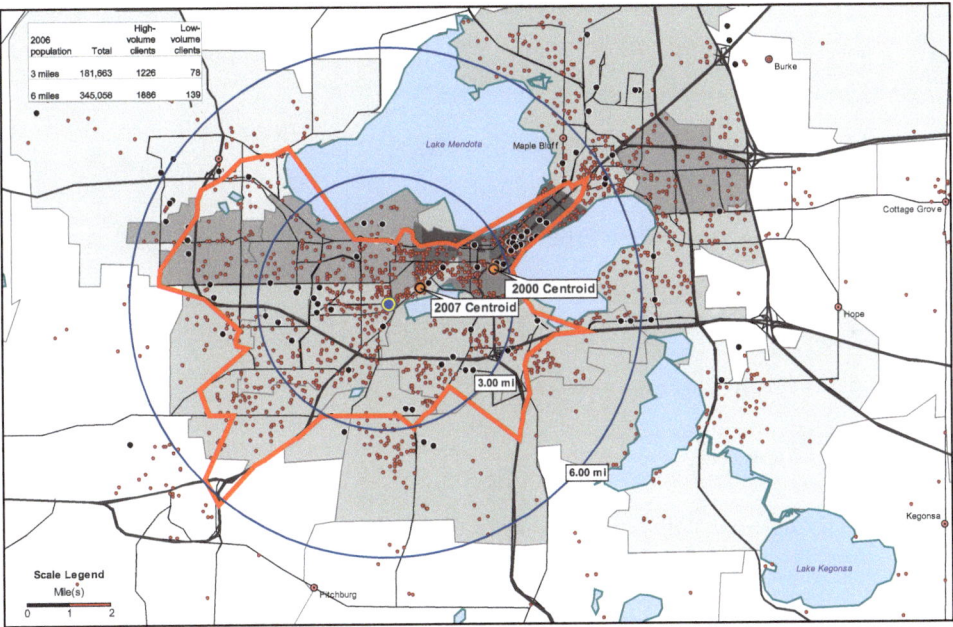

Figure 3.3 Multi-layer map

The General Theory of Location Analysis

Leaders can think about location analysis in three "layers" no matter what their industry:

I   Market area
II   Labor pool
III Transportation web

These three layers of information have these "sublayers," all of which can be portrayed on a map. We'll discuss priorities in different industries later. Most organizations already have an enormous amount of useful information that can be mapped and analyzed.

I Market area
- Customer (or patient) demographics
- Customers by type and/or size
- Competitor locations and market area
- Land use trends: growth, traffic, zoning, etc.
- Advertising reach via different media
- Sales territories, trade boundaries, regulatory borders and tax districts

II Labor pool
- Staff demographics and staff by type
- Competitive employers
- Quality of life: schools, healthcare, crime, etc.
- Cost of living: housing, taxes, utilities, food costs, etc.
- Commute patterns, congestion, parking and public transportation
- Amenities: restaurants, child care, etc.

III Transportation web
- Air, rail, truck, and overnight delivery services and times
- Supplier, vendor and warehousing locations and routes
- Traffic planning, congestion and pedestrian patterns
- Communications infrastructure

Pattern-Seeking Analysis

What does one do with all this information once it's mapped? All analysis is the science and art of seeing new patterns, so the simple first steps are to take the time to study the patterns in the data, ask more questions, find new information, and refine the maps and tables. In short, one needs to answer the basic analytical questions:

- What are the patterns? Are they strong or weak?
- Are we sure the data are accurate?
- Who else has seen something like this?
- What's missing?
- What has changed? What will change? Why?

Like spreadsheets or business graphics, no single perspective holds a complete solution. For example, while one of the most important issues in location analysis is to predict market share, market share is not just about demographics or competitor positioning: it's as much about service or product quality, marketing and sales effectiveness, changing competitor initiatives, and price.

Similarly, a decision about where to locate a building, for example, is not just a geographic decision: decision-makers need to consider land and building costs, financing, production cost implications, and so on.

It is easier to look at what exists than to predict the future, but it's only by seeking and analyzing patterns of facts can leaders can inform their judgment about how people will behave in a particular location. Maps provide clarity and generate better and better questions.

Other Geographic Information

Maps and aerial photography help answer questions about in which country, state, county, or neighborhood one should locate. A high resolution aerial photography or satellite image can bring location analysis to life (figure 3.4). If one's market area is fairly

Figure 3.4 Aerial view of the Lincoln and Washington monuments.

small and the audience well acquainted with the area, seeing familiar features engages their imagination and makes it easier to understand the cartographic information (points, lines, and symbols). The availability and usability of this kind of information is becoming simple. Google Earth is one such service.

Another set of questions about facility location concern the site itself. At this level, one must evaluate visibility, vehicular access, pedestrian access, attractiveness of the building and landscape, and perhaps zoning and other regulations. It helps to make a table like figure 3.5, below, then grade alternative sites in the neighborhood to which the location analysis maps have led.

	SITE CHARACTERISTICS	Site A	Site B (3 is high)	Site C
PRIORITY FACTORS	Visibility	2	3	3
	Position in community / market	2	2	2
	Safety and security	3	3	2
	Access by in-bound commuters	2	3	3
	Access by out-bound commuters	2	3	3
	Local traffic signals	2	3	3
	Congestion: rush	2	3	2
	Congestion: non-rush	2	3	2
	Competitive positioning	2	2	2
	Site circulation	3	3	2
	Pedestrian access	3	2	1
	Attractiveness	3	3	1
	Zoning	2	3	3
	Local advertising coverage	3	2	2
	Local parking	2	2	2
	Public transportation	3	1	0
	Land use planning and trends	2	1	2
	Local amenities	3	2	3
	Total score (54 maximum):	**43**	**44**	**38**

Figure 3.5 Site selection matrix

Data Gold and Garbage

The basic idea of this book is that location (and financial) analysis must be fully integrated with the design of the building. It is just as mistaken to pick a location before considering the building as it is to begin to design a building without having considered the location dynamics. The data has to be right, but there are many sources of location information that leaders, planners, and architects can use to map their world.

Internal Sources

Most organizations already have the most useful and accurate data:

- Customer data bases
- Contact management systems
- Payroll systems
- Accounts payable files (for vendor locations and purchase volumes)

Sharing simple maps of this powerful information is terrific planning and communications. It is rare to see this information portrayed accurately. Executives and salespeople can have a skewed idea of their geography: they remember most the largest or most problematic customers.

> A key technical point in making a map is "geocoding," which requires street addresses in the data base to be accurate.

Public Sources

The United States government makes available huge amounts of information from the 10-year census and other research. Some of this information can be downloaded and applied directly, some sites have maps and tables that can be used as-is. Websites to explore are:

- Bureau of Labor Statistics (www.bls.gov)
- National Atlas (www.nationalatlas.gov)
- American FactFinder (www.factfinder.census.gov)

Each state provides different types and quality of geographic information. Most have census files that can be downloaded into a database or spreadsheet which can then be mapped. Healthcare information is often the most available. Searching the Internet for "Wisconsin population statistics" returns tables of population projections by county. Many cities have a geographic information system (GIS) department which can be a useful resource.

Data Warehouses

There are firms that sell industry-specific and easily used data, having massaged governmental data and their own primary research into a more usable form. Software stores sell "yellow pages" on CD, including business and credit data organized by SIC code and by address, but it's much easier to use maps prepared by a vendor or from a mapping function at the data site than to incorporate it directly into one's own mapping software. One good general data warehouse is www.esri.com.

Primary Research

Every process needs a system of checks and for business mapping the best check is to drive around the neighborhood being studied, even it it's familiar. Nothing can replace seeing first hand the quality of the buildings, observing the people, and testing for the ease of travel.

It's also helpful to interview local planners and economic developers to discuss the developments that will affect populations, transportation, and the character of the area. Some areas are growing so quickly that analyses based on long-term trends are inaccurate.

Industry Specifics

It was said earlier that there are the three basic layers of information—market area, labor pool, and transportation web—useful to leaders and architects when planning any building. This section considers location analysis for several industries and readers are encouraged to learn from others.

Healthcare

A hospital often has many very different geographic markets and, as we saw at the beginning of this section, older location analyses have been dangerously misleading (see pages 18 and 19). The geographic market or service area for oncology, cardiology, family medicine, and women's health can be very different because the networks of referral points are often very different. A hospital's primary and specialty care submarkets are likely to behave differently and have different location sensitivities: a parent locating a clinic for their child's earache is going to make a different buying choice than the dangerously ill cancer patient.

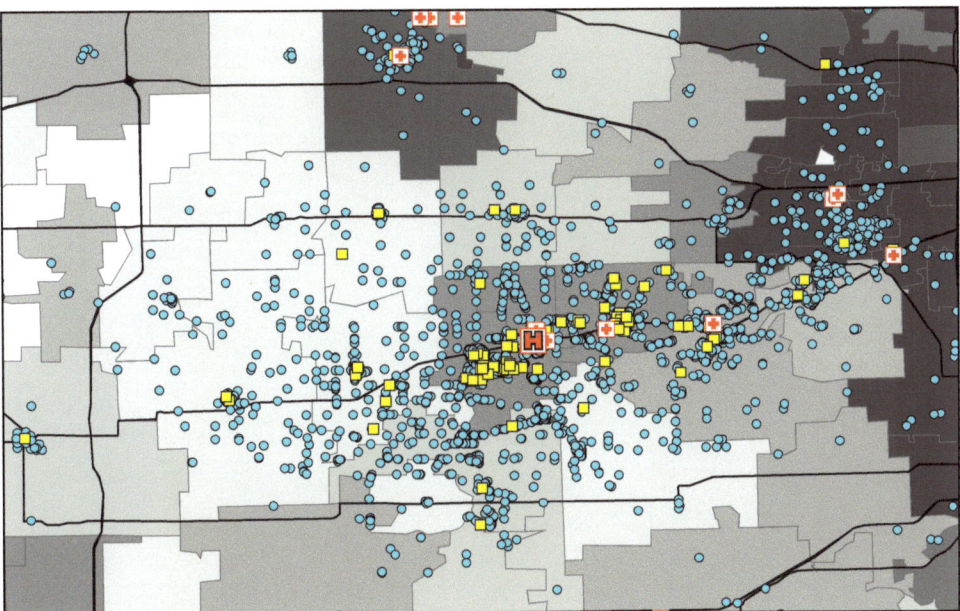

Figure 3.6 Scatter map — healthcare

This leads to another common mistake is giving too much importance to the demographics near the hospital. It is the demographics around the points of referral that matter.

Another surprise to many administrators is that a hospital has four widely different labor pools. Physicians, nurses, administrators, and support staff often decide where to work using different location criteria. Again, a four-layer scatter map will reveal the critical patterns. Administrators may also see a geographic pattern of volunteer and donor locations. These analyses, perhaps aided with an aerial or satellite image, can provide a powerfully revealing perspective on a hospital's community connections.

Another obvious mapping application is for emergency response. A map of patient addresses segregated by referrals and emergency department admissions can shape volume projections which in turn affect not only facility planning, but also staffing plans, wellness initiatives, and so forth.

Many hospitals can easily find internal and external data about health trends and epidemiology in their market area. Each state's human services department offers some level of information. These databases can often be downloaded for free; a staff analyst with some database proficiency can avoid the high cost of re-packaged data from a third-party source (who gets it from the same place).

Retail

Different retailers put different priorities on the market, labor, and transportation layers of their locations: an independent coffee shop will have different location dynamics than a "big box" or a destination store. The scale of location analysis might vary from a neighborhood of one square mile to an entire city or metropolitan area.

Still, the steps of analysis are the same for retailers as for other users. One needs to capture street addresses—perhaps from a newsletter mailing list or from an accounts receivable file to make a customer scatter map. Labor availability is always important but usually less so for smaller stores. Transportation can mean different things depending on scale: it's often revealing to draw a polygon around a small store that represents a 15-minute walk. And again, a satellite image, perhaps with competitors and complementary stores, can help planners get a feel for their customer base. Insets of photographs of competitors can also give focus.

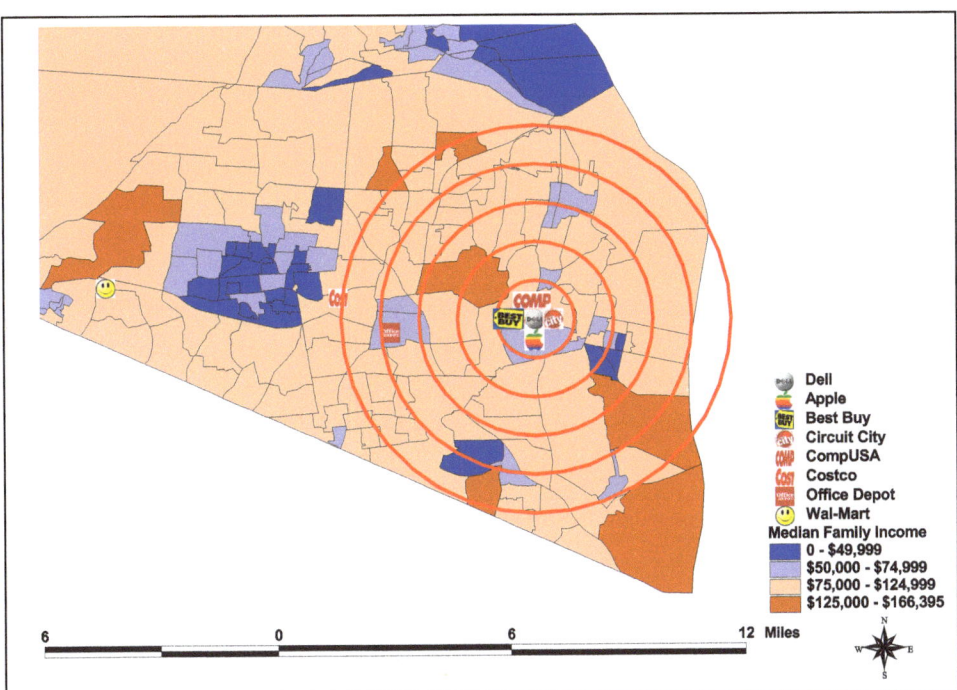

Figure 3.7 Store location analysis

Banking

Banks, credit unions, and savings and loans benefit from their enormous databases of consumer and commercial customer information. They can geographically plot sales volumes for all kinds of credit and deposit relationships and transactions, though online banking services and call centers are diluting this somewhat. Many urban bank branches have a surprisingly small market area. Branch staff tend to remember the customers who talk about having come a long way, but the routine, local visits, and transactions make up the bulk of the business volume.

Like healthcare, the financial institutions often have available a lot of information about competitor market share which can aid in making facility location and sizing decisions.

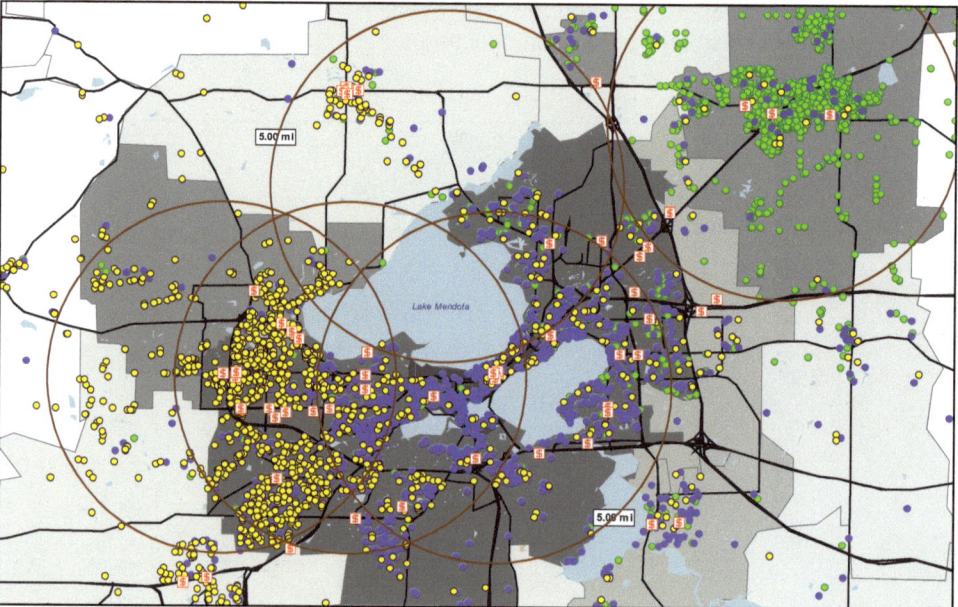

Figure 3.8 Wisconsin bank branch analysis

Education

Distance learning, homeschooling, continuing education, diversity initiatives, and internships in the community have greatly increased the complexity of a school or university's geography. The Internet allows students to participate from—and remain in—places quite distant from the school building. This dynamic directly affects outreach and recruitment and therefore the building's business case. Institutions of education, like healthcare, have very different labor pools: faculty, administrators, and support staff often come from very different places.

"Town-Gown" issues remain important. A large institution has a profound effect on its community's economy, culture, and reputation. There are often strong practical, geographic connections: demographics, housing, transportation systems, taxation, infrastructure, and the distribution of health and emergency services. Maps with overlays of land use and transportation plans can help education and municipal planners collaborate.

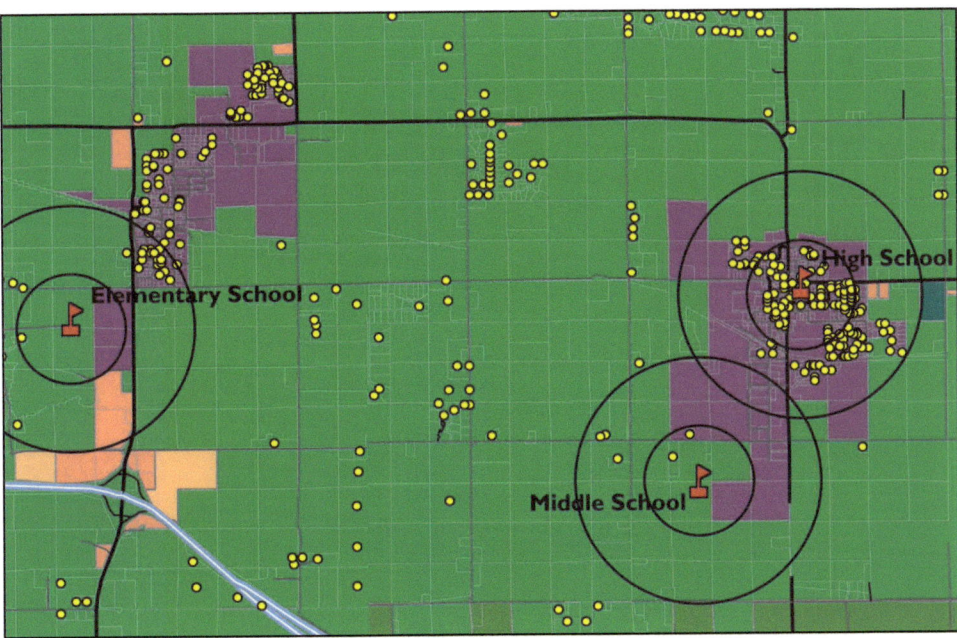

Figure 3.9 K–12 school district access

Manufacturing and Distribution

Manufacturers and distributors need to think about the geographic, logistical links among customers, themselves, and their suppliers. Large manufacturers like an auto company have complex geographic networks among their warehouses, assembly, and final manufacturing plants, and often use many modes of transportation. The simple mapping tools referred to in this paper can illustrate the links, but there are more sophisticated tools—and consultants—to optimize the mix of locations, routes, facility size and type, labor use, and production time.

A distributor like Lands' End may put a geographic priority on its labor pool. Other large manufacturers and distributors have placed plants in rural locations not just because land is cheap, but because they've learned how to tap a hard-working labor force.

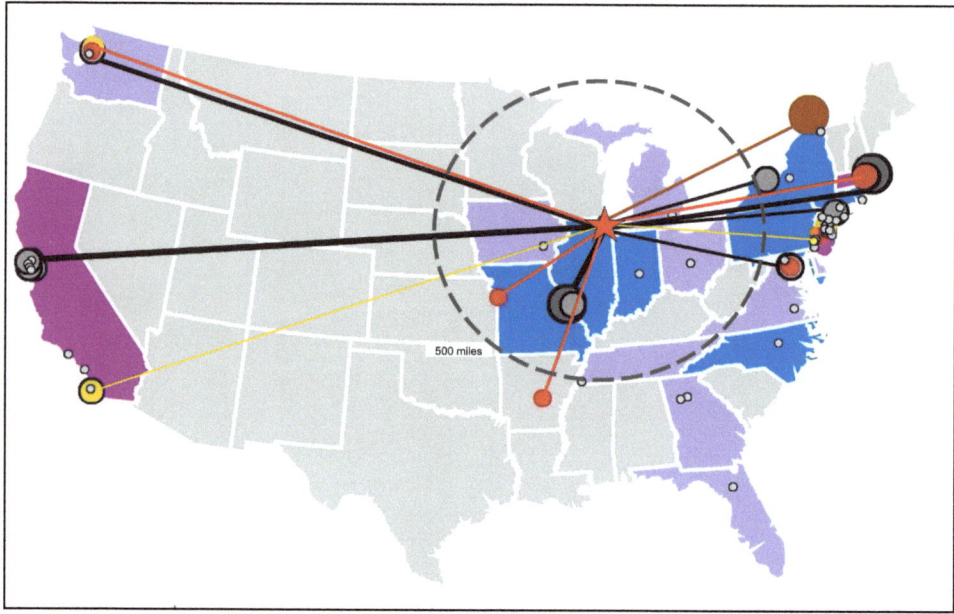

Figure 3.10 Manufacturer/distributor transport web

Business Services

Accounting, law, and consulting firms are less location sensitive than other kinds of businesses. The priorities are usually the access by high paid staff and the availability of amenities. Client access can be important, too, either by car or through an airport. Because their work is intangible, making and reinforcing a positive image is important and affects site decisions. The site selection matrix described earlier (figure 3.5 on page 24) is a good tool for zeroing in on the best place to have one's office.

This is a scatter map of a consulting firm's clients and associates and helps the principals allocate their time meeting clients and reaching their professional network.

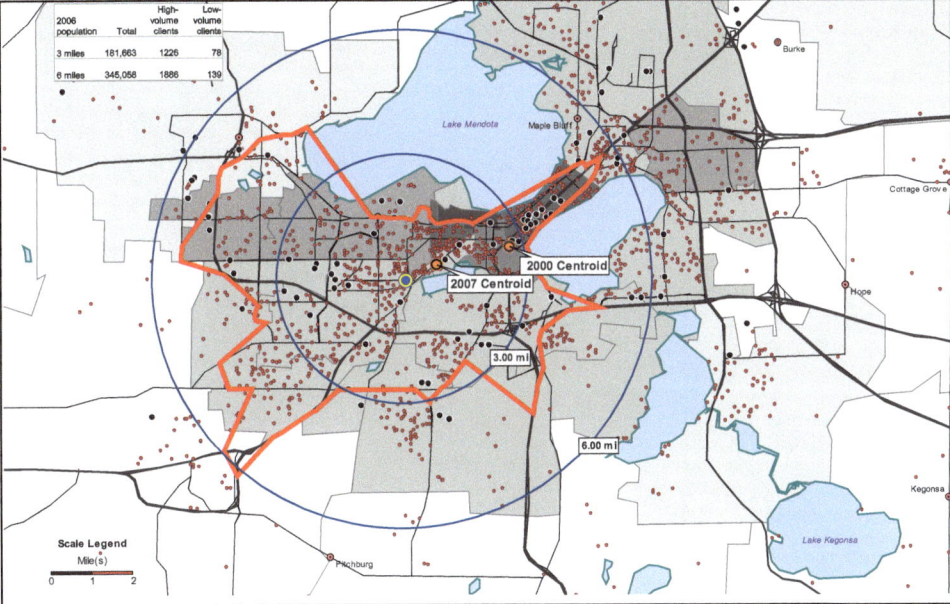

Figure 3.11 Service firm client access

Social Services

The Goodman Community Center in Madison, Wisconsin faced a complex geographic question when considering a new facility. It had very different "customers," including seniors, parents with young children in daycare programs, and teens that walked, biked, and drove to and from the Center at different hours. The Center has a fleet of vans as part of its own transportation system; it also had to consider the routes of public buses, school buses, and the ease of driving and access for people with disabilities. Another layer of the Center's geography was the location of its volunteers and donors, many of whom lived in different neighborhoods than those most needing its vital services, including a food pantry. These maps led to the decision to renovate a 100-year-old factory located at the center of all these forces.

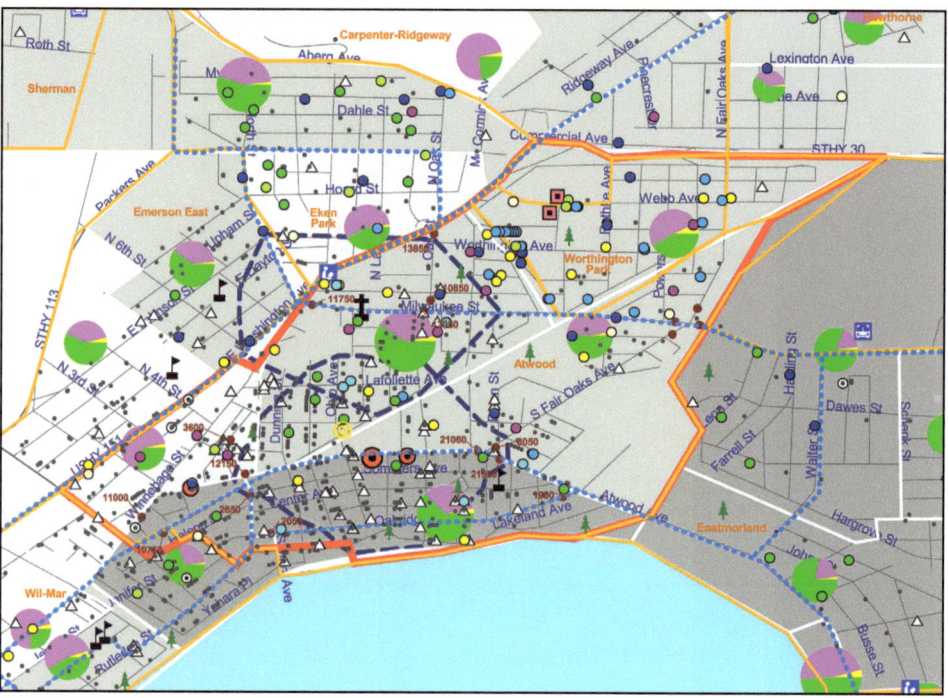

Figure 3.12 Community center service area

Map Design & Art

A map is made up of points, lines, and areas. A *point* can be many things: someone's home, a town, a sales office, or a landmark. A *line* can represent a border, road, bus route, or a flight path, to name a few. An *area* can be a political unit like a state or a neighborhood, or something unique to an organization, like a sales territory or a labor pool.

Points, lines, and areas are given meaning with color, size, symbols, and text. People are amazingly sensitive to the different meanings of a thin or thick line, a dot or square, a blue line or a green line, or a symbol that looks like a house or a blue "H." A dashed line symbolizes something tentative or porous.

A good map uses all these elements to convey important information without distortion. The design of a map is its *cartography,* and it's as much art as science. One can recall very old maps in which the spouting whale in the middle of the "Atlantic Sea" plainly meant a zone of danger and adventure.

Map-Reading Challenges

There are challenges for those new to the study of geography: information quality, spatial ability, irrelevant borders (as ZIP codes can be), and poor cartography.

Information quality: Like any other analysis, the study of location is only as good as the accuracy and the relevance of its data, such as an incomplete or inaccurate customer sales file or an advertiser's exaggeration of media coverage. We discussed information sources earlier. To risk stating the obvious, a map must use information clearly relevant to the issue: one shouldn't use county-level data when block-level data is needed, even if the county data is all that's available.

Spatial ability: One must know one's audience. Some people simply don't understand spatial information as others do. While these people might excel at looking at patterns of numbers or readily absorb what's spoken or written, they can't easily make sense of a map or floor plan or flow diagram. Even for those inclined to map reading, new viewers need time to absorb a map's symbols, colors, lines, scale, and patterns.

Irrelevant borders: Some lines on a map have literal meanings, like a state border, but that doesn't mean that a precise line always conveys precise information. For example, thinking that one's market area is captured perfectly by a circle, county border, or ZIP code edge can be very misleading (pages 18 and 19). Many important decisions have been corrupted by lines on a map.

Poor cartography: A map can easily mislead if it's not designed well. For example, a scatter map of customers will mislead planners if the same size dot is used for a customer who spent $1 as for a customer who spent $1,000. Other common problems are map clutter, unnecessary use of color, and choosing the wrong scale and symbols. This section is all about designing good maps.

Mapping Conventions: North Is Up

Even though the map maker might be intimately familiar with the area under study, it's unsafe to assume others will be. There are certain conventions in map-making that mustn't be forgotten: north is always up. The choices of colors, line weight, and symbols are much more important to maps than in any other analysis. In a spreadsheet—a tool of numerical analysis—graphic presentation is a nice complement but not essential to the information. One might say that with a business map, the graphic presentation *is* the analysis.

Symbols: It was said earlier that even non-cartographers are already attuned to the size, color, and shape of symbols on a map, but if the audience is new to reading maps, it's best to use fewer symbols or create an additional map.

Scale: The map area shouldn't limit the perspective on the issue. Zooming in highlights details which affect the viewer's thinking in one way, when zooming out emphasizes another. Leaders need to look at both scales.

> A "large scale map" is of a small area, and a "small scale map" is of a large area. "Large scale" could mean "one inch = one mile" (1 in. / 1 mi.), versus a "small scale" map of a much wider area, with a scale of 1 in. / 100 mi.

Title: Even the seemingly mundane map title is a design element. It shouldn't be too large, shouldn't be in color, and mustn't have a font that draws undue attention to itself. Maps should always be dated so changes can be tracked over time.

Legend: A mark of a good map is the brevity of its legend: the map should explain itself as much as possible. Like the title, the legend shouldn't distract from the map's contents. A good legend must be easily seen and read. The legend in the map on the next page is long, but conveys essential information.

Insets: An inset is another image (often a locator map, table, text box, or business graphic) that complements the bigger map. Like all graphic design, the size, color, and content of the inset should not distract from the design of the bigger map nor should it be an attempt to make an entirely different point. A good inset complements both the design and content of the presentation.

Location: The Science and Art of Place   37

Call outs: A call out is like a thought balloon in a cartoon: a small bubble or box of text with a leader line to some feature. Map purists think putting words onto the map means the map is poorly designed, but a call out can include essential text or numbers that eliminates the need for another piece of paper.

Figure 3.13 A well designed, though dense, map

Cartographic Tips

Edward Tufte (www.edwardtufte.com) has written brilliantly about using graphics to communicate. His cardinal rule is to *use nothing that has no meaning.* He detests graphics that simply jolly up unimportant information.

1. Each map should make *one* big point.
2. Don't assume the audience reads maps easily, even of their own town.
3. It's OK to include some features as reference points.
4. Every color should have a meaning, otherwise use gray or white.
5. Use gray to show scales such as population density by ZIP code.
6. When displaying an area using color, don't add a line around it.
7. Use the thinnest lines possible.
8. Be careful about what information is layered on top of another.
9. Use an inset map to relate to a much larger or smaller area.
10. When in doubt, leave it out.

Analytical Tools

A map is a form of analysis because it reveals new and useful patterns of information. As we've seen, even simple color scale and scatter maps can be very illuminating, but there are more sophisticated techniques for exploring those patters. Adding circles, drive time polygons, and centroids can raise more and more interesting questions.

Color scale: (See figure 3.14, below) This familiar technique uses shaded areas to represent different data densities, such as a state map with the counties in different gradations of color to represent population densities. (The technical term is a chloropleth map.) While very useful, the reader is again warned not to take the sharp edges of a ZIP code or political boundary as precise border. In truth, the underlying data always change gradually from one side of the boundary line to the other. There are techniques now that show these data changes using gradients blurring from one color into another—but these can take time to read comfortably. An effective compromise is to shade small areas, such as census block groups.

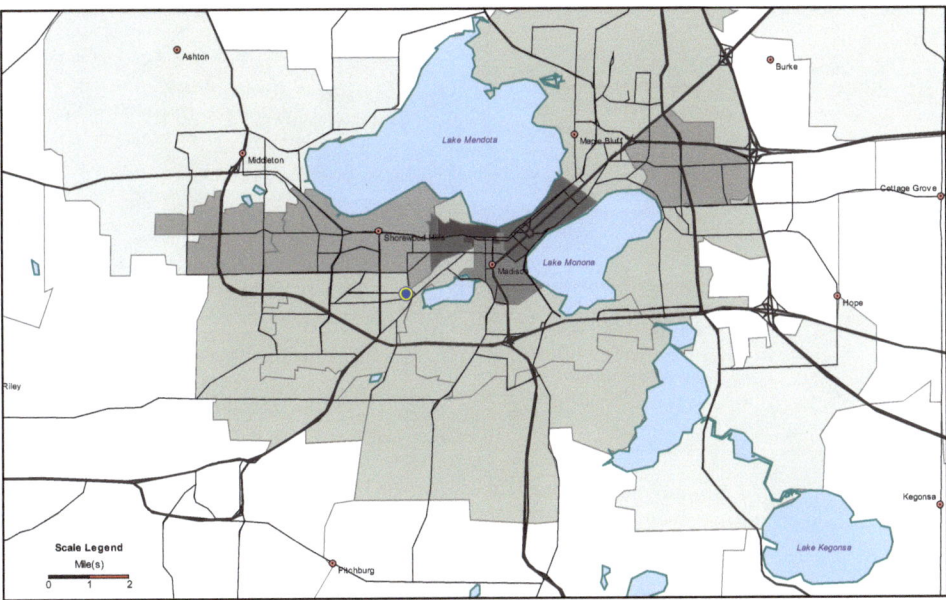

Figure 3.14 Layer 1 of 4: demographics base map

Scatter map: The real power of the new mapping tools is to create scatter maps based on some population's (customers, patients, staff, etc.) addresses. Unlike pushing pins into a street map, the new tools can deal with large numbers, group subpopulations, link to changing databases, and run statistical analyses based on other data associated with the scatter. For example, one can now posit a market border, "lasso" all the addresses (scatter points) within that border, then return to the underlying database to tabulate, say, customer types and counts, total sales, and sales mix by product.

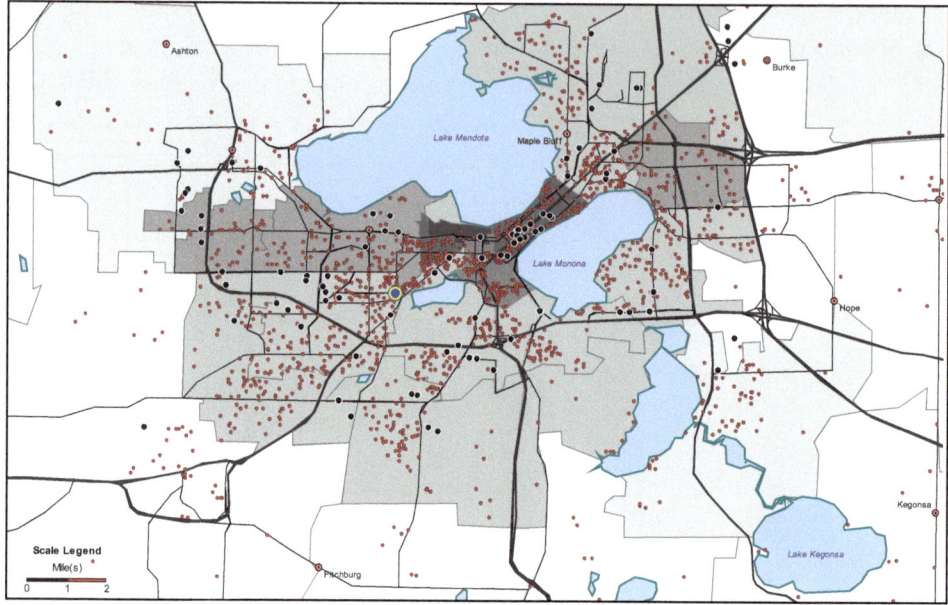

Figure 3.15 Layer 2 of 4: customer scatter map

Circle: It's an accepted practice to draw a circle on a map to answer a question like, "How many customers could we reach within a 3-mile radius of this location?" The problem is that this assumes that travel to or from the center point is equal in all directions, or that the demographics or psychographics (meaning shopping or other behavioral pattern) is also uniform throughout that circle. Still, a simple circle might be a good first step for pursuing a hunch to be carefully analyzed later with a scatter map, centroids or drive time polygons, described on the next page.

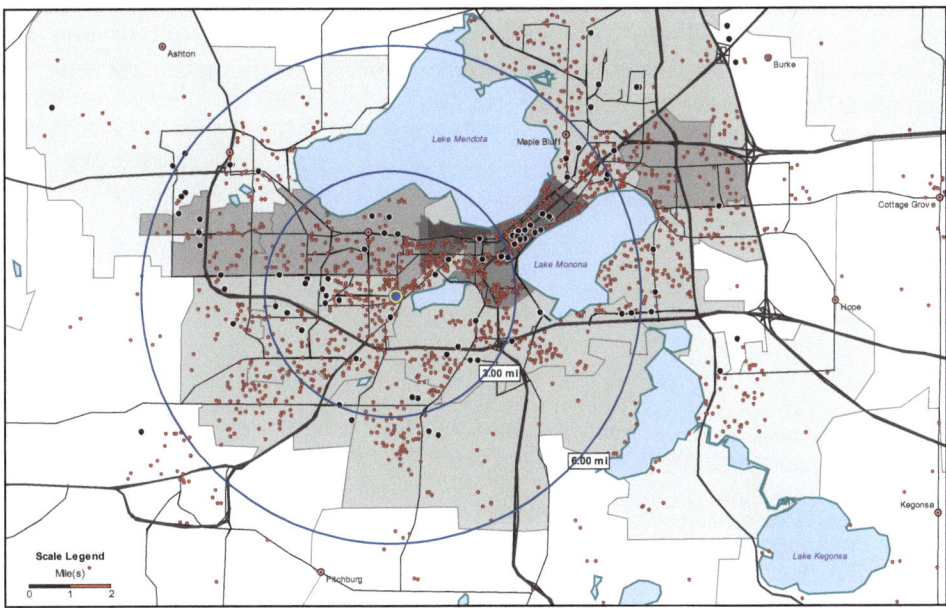

Figure 3.16 Layer 3 of 4: circles to add focus

Drive time polygon: (See map below) Even the simpler mapping programs can create a drive time polygon, which traces the limits of travel to and from a given location based on the speed limits on different road types. Some software allows some adjustment of those speeds to anticipate rush-hour congestion, but it's wise to compare what the computer generates with local knowledge.

Centroid: (See map below) A centroid is the geographic center of a collection of points. While the simpler software cannot calculate a centroid, it is a valuable point of reference for decisions about location. Discussing why a centroid has shifted from one year to another can raise valuable questions about the forces at work on one's marketing, staffing, and transportation initiatives.

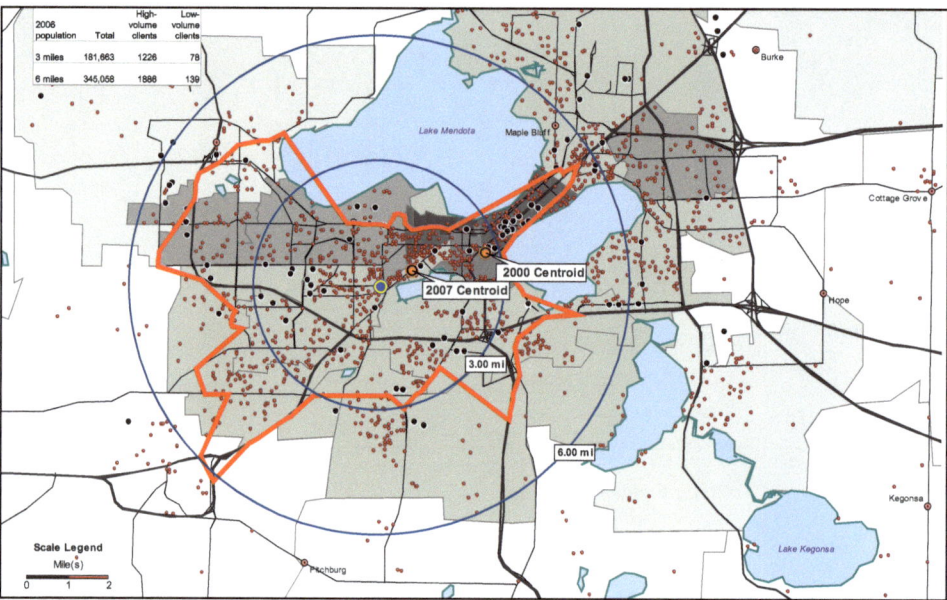

Figure 3.17 Layer 4 of 4: Drive time and market shift

Presenting Maps

When a location issue cannot be shown on a single map, the map maker must think carefully about the sequence of his or her multi-page analysis. Is the audience adept at reading maps? Is the information particularly complex? Are the conclusions radical? What will be the venue and format? A map printed at high resolution is more effective than a projected slide or web map. This is of course different from presenting a spreadsheet or simple business graphics.

The previous section shows how to present complex information by taking advantage of a computer map's "layers" of information. The bottom layer is often the street grid, the next might be the shaded areas of the most relevant demographic information, followed by the largest scatter map, and so forth. These layers can be added or removed with a click. Some tips to aid one's presentation are:

1. Use the highest resolution possible.
2. Put landmarks (one's headquarters, a river, or main road) on the "base" layer and keep them visible. Confirm the audience's understanding of the geography.
3. Make the legend and map scale easily readable, using only key information.
4. Begin with the most certain information like the scatter maps, and then build more complex or speculative layers (circles, centroids, drive times, etc.).
5. Use aerial or satellite images as the base layer or as an inset.
6. Add the call-outs and interpretive insets last.
7. Don't treat the maps as sacred: set an example by drawing on one with a big marker.

Trends: If one has the data, it can be illuminating to see how the pattern of the top 20% of one's customers has shifted—or not shifted—over several years. Clicking back and forth through these layers/years can make a dramatic point about the effectiveness of one's marketing campaigns and sales management. These patterns support the critical projection of sales, which defines the building's size and scale of investment. The same technique can be used to study changes in staff locations and labor pools.

Consistency and conventions: If maps are new to the audience, it is worth taking extra care to create conventions for each map's lines, colors, and symbols. This will help immeasurably when creating each year's maps.

Recap, Resources and First Steps

"Without geography, you're nowhere." – Jimmy Buffett

Maps and other location information, no matter what the organization's size or industry, can help make many important managerial decisions besides a building's location. While location analysis has its limitations, every leader should know what external forces will shape, strengthen, and threaten their building.

Resources

Microsoft's MapPoint software is a good way to begin one's own location analysis, though ESRI's BusinessMap provides some richer features for beginning users. Maptitude, MapInfo, and ESRI's ArcGIS suite are more sophisticated tools. Other GIS (geographic information systems) are being developed and some websites provide simple mapping tools online. Data sources have already been discussed at length. There is a GIS community and one can search the Internet for GIS software and consultants and find blogs and ezines. It's a high-tech community and web-friendly. Many universities have GIS departments or less formal groups that host portal pages.

Action

1. Assign someone to learn the software and become the in-house expert.
2. Research data sources and bookmark useful URLs.
3. Create a customer scatter map with differentiators like sales volume or type.
4. Decide the scale or area of the map by looking at the first scatter maps.
5. Create a scatter map of all staff distinguished as exempt or non-exempt.
6. Create another scatter map (using a different symbol) of 6 top competitors.
7. Use a simple gray background theme by ZIP code of population density.
8. Present several maps to senior managers and brainstorm ten great questions.
9. Keep a gallery of maps, organized by market, labor, and transportation.
10. Experiment!

The powerful new management science of geography will substantially improve your ability to build the right building at the right time… in the right place.

A Reflection on Community

Our discussion so far has been about understanding an organization's location, its place in a market or service area, access to labor, and its fit within a transportation web. But there are other, perhaps deeper issues in location decisions. With new powers come new responsibilities, and leaders should stop and think about how their location decisions affect other people.

A well-run organization clearly benefits its community with stability, new jobs, purchases of local supplies and services, and a profound local economic multiplier from all the living costs of a successful workforce. Clearly, it's good when a leader invests in a community, but it's bad when they divest, even if the long-term benefit is the organization's survival and growth.

A community is more than jobs and a marketplace. It is a sense of place and a feeling of belonging that is part of human nature and essential to happiness. Who doesn't believe that the place in which they grew up profoundly affected their character? Our sense of community—a vital part of our self-identity—is threatened by the Internet, increasing mobility, and all the economic forces creating sprawl.

P.J. O'Rourke wrote, "Cities are the mess people make getting rich." This may be strong, but it is true that the overseas factories that supply us with material things are not always safe or healthy. Breaking down borders through trade agreements can promote economic growth everywhere but can we care enough about places we don't see?

One of a leader's most powerful and lasting decisions is choosing where to build a new building. It's obvious that an efficient building with room to grow and the flexibility to change is good for everyone; relocation, even across town, stresses the community. A building standing vacant because it was poorly planned not only deprives the community of an economic benefit, but it is ugly and therefore dispiriting. It discourages others from investing nearby.

Every situation in which leaders find themselves differs in its ethical issues and importance. We trust the reader will use the power of geography to help the world be a better place.

4 · Finance: Easy Analysis vs. Hard Decisions

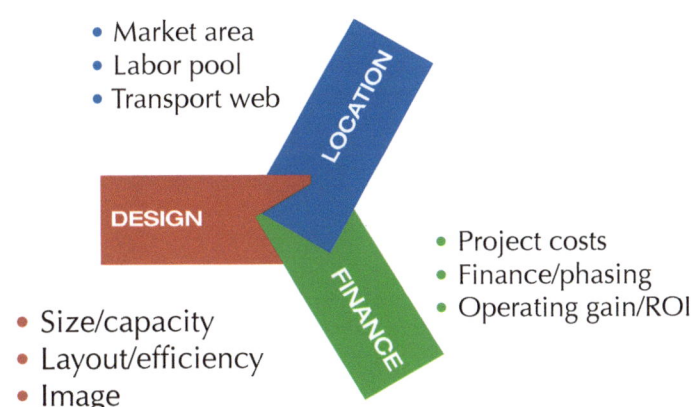

There are three critical finance questions about buildings linked directly to their location and design:

- What does the project cost to build and to occupy?
- What's the best way to pay for it?
- How will each alternative affect financial performance?

This section helps the reader take the highest-level view of a building's financial issues. We leave it to others to address the many project financing techniques in different industries.

Myths & Heresy

The author, who has an M.B.A. in finance, has learned through experience there are five dangerous myths about financial analysis that can take leaders over career-destroying cliffs. But the key problem is this: *The two major benefits of a building project can rarely be quantified precisely.* The two biggest numbers in these analyses are changes to revenue and to payroll, and these derive from the leader's intuitive judgments of how the building and its location will affect market share and productivity in 5 to 10 years.

There's no escaping that the biggest assumptions are more leadership vision than scientific calculation. Long spreadsheets and return calculations out to three decimal places provide a false precision that has doomed many projects.

Benjamin Franklin rightly warned us to "beware small expenses" because they can accumulate dangerously. But first one needs the tough judgment calls about the basic business issues.

Myth #1: It's important to get the least expensive real estate

Of course, everyone should get a good deal. But a sensitivity analysis correlating land or construction costs to overall financial performance almost always shows that a 10% variation in cost has little effect on operating margin.

The point here is not to ignore the real estate costs whether leasing or owning, but to keep them in their proper financial perspective. It's wrong to give too much time to the deal-making and not enough to the basic opportunities: even a 1% gain in market share or productivity (meaning, a reduction in direct cost per unit) is a huge annual gain— and larger gains are often possible with the right location and design.

Myth #2: Off-balance sheet financing makes a project

If clever and complex financing is needed to make a project viable, it's best to stop and revisit its basic economics. A sensible idea is to begin the project planning by assuming traditional mortgage financing or leasing at market rates—and then use other techniques to enhance or guarantee the return. Beware of the transaction costs in complex financing. Legal fees, banking fees, executive time, audit risk, and board confusion can substantially dilute the value of these schemes. The real benefit of these techniques may not be interest expense savings, but increased financial flexibility.

In the end, a complex financing scheme may indeed be needed to get a project off the ground, but it's not where to start. Of course the most common form of off-balance sheet financing is leasing, a section about which is provided below.

Myth #3: Discounted cash flow models have all the answers

Many analysts take as gospel that multi-year discounted cash flow models like Net Present Value and Internal Rate of Return yield solid comparisons of dissimilar project investments.

There have always been technical problems with these analyses. The first is about the nature of the discount rates themselves. The discount rate is the sum of a) some risk-free rate of return (usually T-bills), b) a predicted rate of inflation, and c) some risk premium. Can anyone say with a straight face they can confidently predict these over 10 years? Warren Buffett can't. What's more, an average discount rate is useless: the present value changes radically if the real discount rate spikes early or late in the planning horizon.

Another problem is the choice of planning horizon. What good is a 10-year analysis if revenue and payroll cannot be predicted with any confidence after 3 years? Those last 7 columns are not just worthless, but misleading.

It's already been shown that the final question in the financial analysis of a facility project is not "What is the Net Present Value?" but rather "What will our financial statements look like in the future?" See below for another approach.

Myth #4: Industry benchmarks are safe targets

While accounting firms, hospitals, and a few other well-organized or regulated industries have facility performance information, there are otherwise few industry benchmarks. It's amazing how similar organizations in the same industry in the same markets will use facilities so differently.

One should know how top competitors use their buildings, their largest fixed asset. A staff member should map, photograph, and study municipal records about their functionality, image, quality, and capacity.

Myth #5: Builders knows what projects cost

A common mistake is to ask a builder what, say, an office building costs and then simply add the cost of land and 20% to cover fees. The more developed and detailed the design, the better the estimate. Better still if the site is known: changes in topography, soil composition, and utility connections can mean large cost differences. Many reputable builders provide what are called pre-construction services: estimating, reviewing scheduling and constructability, and value engineering.

Good cost information is of course valuable if one understands the assumptions behind the numbers. A budget should be an educational and project management tool. Without enough detail, there's no opportunity to make reallocation decisions or anticipate tasks and capital demands. Figure 4.1 on the next page is a budget form proven successful on projects of all kinds.

These are five myths about financial analysis. Now we can turn to fresh approaches that can help leaders make and present confident forecasts about their building project's financial performance.

Project Budget Gross Square Feet (GSF): 145,139

SOURCES OF FUNDS		AMOUNT	COMMENTS	% of Total
First Mortgage		$11,924,422	See Debt Service Schedule	78.1%
Equity	15.0%	2,249,898	Of Closing, Soft, Building Costs	14.7%
Ground Lease		0	Or other secondary debt	0.0%
F, F & E Purchases (Cash)	100%	975,000	Furniture, Fixtures & Equipment	6.4%
F, F & E Leases		0	Balance of F,F&E	0.0%
Government Incentives		0	$1MM possible	0.0%
Cash		114,000	Planning and start-up costs	0.7%
TOTAL SOURCES		**$15,263,320**		100.0%

USES OF FUNDS	NUMBER OF UNITS	UNIT PRICE	BUDGET	COMMENTS
PLANNING COSTS				
Consulting Fee			$87,000	
Other			0	
Subtotal			$87,000	Can be capitalized
COSTS TO CLOSING				
Accounting Fees			$13,000	Cost segregation, pro forma
Appraisal			4,500	
Environmental Surveys			3,000	Phase I
Financing Costs		1.0%	25,000	To be negotiated
Legal Fees			10,000	Land, loan, entity
Soil Borings/Testing			12,500	
Surveys			7,000	Estimate from architects
Title Insurance			2,500	
Subtotal			$77,500	
SOFT COSTS				
Construction Interest		9.0%	$395,635	Soft + Hard Costs, X 7/12 X 50%
Project Management Fee			175,000	
Design Fees		6.2%	650,000	Base contract + landscaping, etc.
Insurance, Permits			5,000	Owner's Risk, Liability
Interim Real Estate Taxes			0	
Contingency		10.0%	122,564	
Subtotal		$9.29	$1,348,199	
HARD COSTS				
Acquisition	18,112	$60.73	$1,100,000	90% of asking price
Site Development			275,000	Utilities, grading
Renovation	18,112	$54.00	978,048	
Expansion	127,027	$72.50	9,209,458	Blended cost for office, warehouse
Racking System			150,000	50% reuse
Processing Equipment			75,000	25% reuse
Office Furniture	50,000	$15.00	750,000	50% reuse
Data/Phone Wiring	127,027	$0.50	63,514	Wireless distribution
Contingency		10.0%	1,122,602	
Subtotal			$13,723,621	
START-UP COSTS				
Relocation			$17,000	Per mover estimate
Marketing			10,000	Ads, promotions
Subtotal			$27,000	
TOTAL USES	Cost/s.f.:	$105.16	**$15,263,320**	

Figure 4.1 Project budget.

Forecasts, Flexibility and Lease vs. Own

The critical analytical question is how will having a certain building in a certain place at a certain time affect a) market share, b) cost of labor and materials per unit of output, and c) direct facility expenses. While one can't calculate these first two directly, one can reach a confident conclusion by thoroughly examining the common sense of each project concept. Figure 4.2 shows how to pull these big questions together and help make those difficult long-term forecasts.

FINANCIAL PERFORMANCE IMPROVEMENTS		
REVENUE	Market share	%
Rationale: Visibility, sales management, customer access	Product revenue	
	Service revenue	
		$100
COST OF GOODS SOLD	Direct labor	
Rationale: Workflow, morale, supplier access, shipping costs, utilities	OT labor	
	Raw materials	
	Shipping	
	Inventory costs	
		$70
OVERHEAD	Supervisory labor	
Rationale: Centralization, facility financing, standardization	Facilities	
	Interest expense	
	Depreciation	
	Taxes	
		$10
PROFIT (LOSS) / SF		$20

Figure 4.2 ROI worksheet

The location analyses described in Chapter 3 will help leaders understand future market potential. Many businesses have several different markets, some of which may be less sensitive to a facility's location and appearance than others. One has to ask the market share question for each market.

Decision-makers can use building design information (the subject of Chapter 5) to inform their judgment about productivity improvements. How a building affects output can be broken down into labor and material costs. A building should optimize productivity with streamlined layouts, equipment use, and work design. Facility expenses are the easiest to calculate, but lower is not necessarily better if the result is a loss of flexibility (see below), poor quality, or balance sheet distortions.

Remember the Small eExpenses

One can and should consider the lesser P&L lines once the effects on revenue and payroll have been estimated. A better building can improve smaller line items such as recruitment costs, returns, utilities, material handling charges, healthcare benefits, and so forth. One distribution company realized that by consolidating warehouses it would save $75 a year in packing tape. While the amount was trivial, it made vivid the benefits of a $10 million project.

Invest in Flexibility

The leader, given their unique access to information, is most aware of the potential for change within and outside their organizations. No one should fault them for pronouncing a confident vision of a certain future while at the same time investing in flexibility. Buildings are certainly hard to change, but flexibility in location, design, and finance can be had.

Locations can be made flexible with lease terms, land options, land banking, and careful site planning. These come with a cost, but a rushed relocation is always more expensive. The building itself can be made flexible with careful space use planning, robust infrastructure, and standardization of structural units and of furniture.

Financing can be made flexible with good lease terms or loan covenants, project phasing, layered financing, and creative techniques including rate swaps, hedging, and purchase options. These are smart investments if they raise the project cost 10% but increase the building's life by 20% or more.

Leasing Versus Owning

It's confusing to think of leasing versus owning as purely a financial decision; there are many qualitative considerations (see the next page). The leader must set priorities to each factor to make a balanced judgment.

Furthermore, the leader may be faced with choosing between leasing one building and owning another. In which case, the first step is to consider all the costs of each alternative making assumptions about lease rates and financing costs, transaction costs, the operating expenses in either scenario (utilities, maintenance, and so forth), and the effects on liquidity that matter at that time in an organization's financial life.

	LEASING	OWNING
Cash Flow	Saving a down payment conserves growth capital. A long-term fixed-rate lease can be better than a variable interest expense.	Owning eliminates landlord's profit from occupancy expense. This savings increases over time.
Amortization	There are no principal payments when leasing.	Amortized loan principal is a type of savings program, regained at sale or useful for later financing.
Tax Advantages	Rent is a large deductible expense.	Depreciation expense provides a near-term tax benefit, some of which can be lost upon sale.
Liquidity	Short-term leases can make it easier to take on other forms of debt.	Ownership limits borrowing power; lenders often view long-term leases as just as illiquid.
Appreciation	An economic downturn could eliminate gains from owning. Leasing has a predictable financial result.	Any appreciation is "free" equity. Ownership of property is an inflation hedge.
Flexibility	Lease options to renew or expand can be useful, if the lease term is not too long.	With enough land, one can expand how and when one wants. *Contractions* are difficult.
Management	Often a professional manager takes on these headaches.	The owner controls upkeep of property, making any improvements they want.
Pride	An intangible benefit. Large tenants can get signage rights and appear as if they own.	Ownership is a symbol of stability to customers, staff and investors.
Quality Control	Tenants must accept a building as it is, but a build-to-suit is a way to lease a "custom" building.	With full control of the development process, the owner ensures details are as they want.

Figure 4.3 Leasing versus owning

Conclusion

In Chapter 2, we learned to use a one-page scorecard (below) to summarize the project's costs and benefits. This puts the critical finance decisions in their proper perspective. Leaders will need to evolve their financial analysis and financing schemes as the building concept evolves with decisions about location and design.

There's no escaping the tough judgments needed to predict how a building reshapes the financial statements 1, 3, and 10 years after the project is done. The need for flexibility is obvious. All facility decisions are long-term decisions, so it's best to be prepared with good information and not distracted by too-complex forms of analysis. One needs a realistic view of risks and volatility and a team of honest thinkers with different and valuable points of view.

In the next section, we will discuss how to apply the financial model (and location analysis of the previous section) to the design of the building itself.

					Alternatives		
MATCH TO OBJECTIVES		CURRENT		A		B	
	WEIGHT	SCORE / WEIGHTED SCORE					
1 Achieve high visibility within community	3	2	6	4	12	5	15
2 Ensure easy access for customers and staff	5	3	15	4	20	5	25
3 Enhance facility tour from approach through exit	3	2	6	4	12	4	12
4 Size plant for 5-year projections	5	2	10	5	25	4	20
5 Accommodate new inventory and material management	4	2	8	5	20	4	16
6 Provide for added office staff per business plan	4	3	12	5	20	4	16
7 Be able to expand on site by 250% over 10 years	4	1	4	5	20	3	12
8 Provide a safe and healthy work environment	5	3	15	5	25	3	15
9 Ensure easy workflows in all departments	5	1	5	5	25	5	25
10 Enhance on-site access by suppliers	3	2	6	4	12	3	9
11 Locate within overlap of best labor pools	5	1	5	5	25	4	20
12 Improve communications among all groups	5	2	10	5	25	4	20
13 Protect resale value	4	3	12	4	16	5	20
14 Protect access to capital	4	3	12	4	16	5	20
BENEFITS			126		273		245
COSTS							
PROJECT TOTAL ($M)					$16.8		$14.8
ADDED CASH FLOW ($M)					$2.5		$2.3
OCCUPANCY COSTS ($K)					$713		$675

Figure 4.4 Facility scorecard

5 · Design: Practical and Psychological Functions

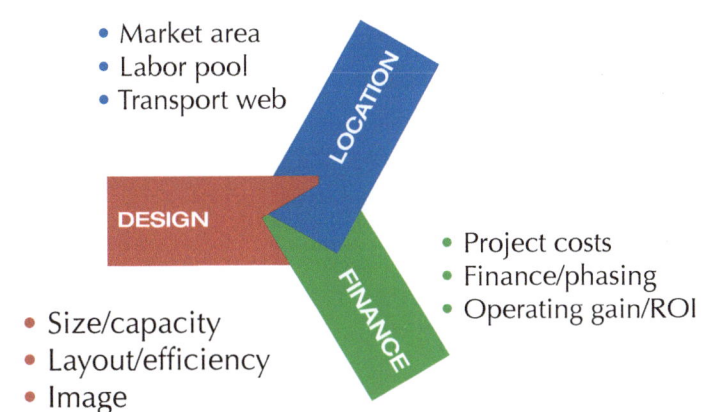

The Key Idea

Form follows function. – Louis Sullivan

Form becomes feeling. – Frank Lloyd Wright

Practical and Psychological Functions

The key idea of this chapter is this: A leader gets a great building only by thinking hard about each *practical* and *psychological* function of architecture's nine elements:

1. Floor plans and transitions
2. Siting, landscaping, and nature
3. Exterior massing and interior volumes
4. Structural materials and colors
5. Windows, light, and rhythm
6. Interior colors and textures
7. Lighting, ventilation, and acoustics
8. Furniture
9. Details, decoration, and art

A church shows how this idea works: the leader and architect, thinking only about the *practical* functions of a church, will predict the number of pews needed, the size of the parking lot, and the capacity of the Sunday School classrooms. They will establish all the liturgical requirements, such as the placement of the altar and pulpit. But a caring leader and a good architect also "energize" the church's *psychological* functions: the need to inspire reverence and community, to respect tradition yet appeal to contemporary worshippers, and to create feelings of safety, joy, and serenity.

Terms, Myths, and Mistakes

What is Architecture?

Before beginning this section, we should arm ourselves with a few definitions. Many architects say what they do is create the *built environment,* meaning all the man-made things that change our world, including roads, bridges, and monuments. It is an intellectual term that may not be helpful to people new to the field.

Architecture is an art, and a building is an artwork. Art is something intellectually and emotionally profound that changes our outlook on life. Art is also subjective: something may affect one person profoundly and another person not at all. The *Mona Lisa* affects everyone and so everyone feels it is art; because it affects everyone so deeply, we consider it great art. Something that is merely clever, shocking, or new is not art.

While a shed, a barracks, or a warehouse could be described as architecture, common sense tells us these mundane things are not works of art, but merely buildings—though Philip Johnson (1906–2005), a notable American architect, designed a fantastic doghouse.

And while a great deal of craft and engineering are needed in building, neither makes a building artistic. However, many people appreciate craftsmanship and engineering and both draw them into a building's architecture.

Design is both a noun and a verb. A workable definition of *design* is "an orderly arrangement of parts." It is enough for a leader to know that design is what an architect does when he or she brings the nine elements together into one… design.

Good Architecture Costs Too Much

Good design does not necessarily raise a building's cost, although good architects should be paid more than bad ones. In fact, good architecture can cost *less* because bad architecture often depends on expensive shapes and materials. The leader must set a realistic budget by thinking through their needs, getting professional assistance, and studying the costs of similar, good buildings. If the leader's only goal is to spend the minimum, then the building probably will not meet his or her needs. Some buildings cost a lot and should never have been built. But some costly buildings are worth every penny: the Wisconsin legislature recently spent $100 million renovating its State Capitol, arguably the most beautiful in the nation (figure 5.30).

This book aims to equip the leader to set an accurate budget based on considered decisions and choices. Any project goes off budget and off schedule when its objectives drift. The leader and the architect should view the budget as a creative challenge.

Good Architecture Takes Too Much Time

If good architecture depends on careful thinking, it follows that good architecture takes longer to create than bad architecture. Most projects fall behind schedule because the executive hesitates to start, putting the architect under unrealistic time pressure. A good leader gives the architect and him- or herself months to discuss, research, create, debate, and refine. Good buildings do take time.

The Owners Can Do What They Please

The American ethos holds that owners can do what they please on their land, but zoning and environmental laws, building codes, and federal safety regulations say otherwise. Mature people accept that with any right comes an equal responsibility, and this is true with property. Every building affects its neighbors, changing their views, casting shadows, adding traffic, affecting property values, and increasing the need for fire and police protection. Good buildings improve the local economy, raise the tax base, spin off local spending, and add competition for workers. Poorly designed buildings do these things poorly. Buildings last longer than those who build them, and bad buildings get abandoned and leave a hole in the community that can take decades to fill.

But many communities are blessed with civic-minded leaders who have moved their organizations downtown to invigorate the local economy. The Italian Renaissance architect Leon Battista Alberti said, "Men of public spirit applaud and rejoice when you have raised a fine wall or portico, and adorned it with fine portals, columns, and a handsome roof, knowing thereby you have not only served yourself, but them, too."

"Creative Heroics"

Architecture, like all art, is a plodding path studded with small flashes of light. Cesar Pelli, one of today's most thoughtful and successful architects, said that the idea of a "hero-architect" who designs a beautiful building in one creative flash is a myth. The leader's first goal should *not* be a masterpiece, but an attractive and efficient building that obviously reflects the organization's spirit. Brilliance is possible only after the basics have been mastered.

Non-revenue-generating Space

Many managers are sure that some spaces generate more revenue than others and so are worth more. That idea misses the mark. Can a store maximize sales without a storeroom? Can a hospital heal the sick without a boiler? Boardrooms are "non-revenue-generating" but appear to be indispensable. No space should be wasted, but all spaces must work together in a comprehensive program, in what architect David Kuffner calls *proactive geometry*.

Wright's Roofs and Ego

Any roof will leak if left untended for 50 years. Frank Lloyd Wright's buildings (a few of which are famous—or infamous—for their leaky roofs) have stood so long because they are among the best in the world. Innovation means taking a few risks. Besides creating new architectural forms, Wright invented many new construction techniques and most worked brilliantly. While Wright was a difficult person—a very difficult person—he was indeed a genius. A strong leader knows that genius can be worth enduring.

Setting Objectives

The most common failure in architecture occurs at the outset: a lack of meaningful objectives. Many huge projects break ground with only vague ideas about the building's purpose. Chapter 2 tells how to set clear and compelling objectives that support the organization's goals. Without a complete statement of objectives for the building, the conversation about practical and psychological functions will totter.

Proof of Leadership

The decisions to build and what to build are lonely decisions and delegating them will not blunt the criticisms of failure. But society is interested in the opposite result: a great building that proves great leadership. The leader can then adopt whatever degree of modesty he or she chooses.

The Nine Elements of Architecture

The facility plan, including detailed location and financial analysis, is the first step in architecture. With strong board support, the facility plan provides direction, confidence, and inspiration, and the leader and the architect can begin to design the building. The early designs always prompt some re-examination of the facility plan; conditions evolve rapidly in this fast-paced world. The plan allows the leader to adapt to change, not be stalled by it. Planner Richard Muther says that the primary purpose of planning is "not to arrive at a predetermined outcome, but to immerse oneself in the issues."

This chapter outlines the practical and psychological functions of each of the nine elements of architecture, framing the critical communication between the leader and architect.

Each of the nine sections discussed here begins with a brief introduction, followed by subsections which outline the important practical and psychological functions common to most buildings. Each section closes by describing the analyses the reader can use to make informed decisions.

This outline of elements seems to suggest that architecture is a linear process; in reality, it is not. It is an organic process, and a good architect can start a successful design at any point with any element. But the organization outlined here is a good, logical way for newcomers and pragmatists to proceed.

Element 1 ▪ Floor Plans and Transitions

The block plan (figure 5.1) was developed in the facility plan, and it is the seed of the floor planning process. A block plan ensures a sensible arrangement of spaces, corridors, and courtyards so the entire building can be efficient and useful. Some great buildings use the least space necessary in the most practical rectangles. Other buildings are made great by using eccentric spaces to fulfill subtle psychological functions. The Oval

Figure 5.1 Block plan

Office is an elegant shape and is an icon of American power. The cruciform of Notre Dame de Paris is not strictly efficient, but praying within the Cross fulfills the cathedral's holy purpose. A spacious hospital lobby lets families compose themselves before visiting a loved one in distress.

Practical Functions

❑ *Reception.* The reception area is the first point of human contact and a security and information checkpoint (figure 5.2). Visitors can get the wrong impression if the reception area is too large or small or if the receptionist's chair is too high or too low. They miss vital information if the displays are out of date or hard to read.

Figure 5.2 Reception desk concept

❑ *Work groups and workflow.* Research shows that six is the best number for a workgroup. Different cultures and ages will tolerate differently sized groups, but an ocean of cubicles is impersonal. Groups do not have to be in their own rooms, but dividers of the right height balance concentration with camaraderie. In addition to workflow, leaders need to consider all that staff and guests see and hear from where they work. Another workflow issue is vertical circulation. A United States Air Force study found that to travel up or down one floor was the same as traveling 100 feet horizontally. The correlation between distance and productive interaction is unique to every organization.

Design: Practical and Psychological Functionality   63

Figure 5.3 Monticello floor plan

❑ *Circulation and wayfinding.* Corridors are necessary evils; it is more efficient and friendlier to move directly from room to room. Getting guests quickly from the entry to their point of business is obviously important. Corridors can consume 20 percent of floor space, but may be enriched with displays and signage: an airport terminal is a kind of super corridor. It is human nature, perhaps part of our survival instinct, to want to be comfortably oriented in an enclosed space. A building's layout should be obvious; wayfinding should depend on signs as little as possible.

❑ *Natural light.* A theme in architecture is the immeasurable benefit of natural light and air. Large rectangular floors are efficient, but the need for natural light and ventilation argues for long, thin shapes. This is one of many trade-offs the leader must balance, but our increasing need for *sustainable design* (the current term for environmentally friendly design and construction) emphasizes the power of light.

❑ *Fitting furniture and equipment.* Floor plans are improved when leaders devote time to detailed furniture and equipment layouts. A cardboard model with toy-size pieces is an effective way to be sure everything fits and flows.

❑ *Expansion paths.* More buildings are too small rather than too large because costs and risk aversion lead executives to scrimp on space and land. Rooms and buildings should be arranged to anticipate known and unknown paths of growth. The first set of floor plans should show how the building could double in size.

❑ *Flexibility.* The leader is the one who can see the threats and trends in every department. A square floor plan with few walls is more flexible than a complex or curved building shape, but it often fails to provide a unique sense of place. The facility plan's statement of objectives (discussed in Chapter 2, "The Facility Plan and Its Business Case"), if well written, provides a helpful ordering of priorities.

❑ *Standardization.* Space usage standards are helpful, but an enlightened leader allows the architect to provide enough floor space to develop a lively variety of work settings.

❑ *Accessibility and regulations.* The Americans with Disabilities Act, OSHA, the local fire department, and zoning ordinances define the sizes and arrangement of many rooms. Some codes dictate how large a building's footprint on a site can be. Not all regulations are sensible in every situation, but it is usually a waste of time to argue for exceptions to the rules.

❑ *Safety.* Dark corners and too many doors make it easier for bad people to hide in or near a building. Dangerous materials or operations need a zone of safety. The leader must consider lines of sight, entry control points, and areas of privacy to allow everyone to work without worry.

❑ *Mechanics and infrastructure.* In addition to the corridors, one should allot 15 percent of floor space for walls, stairwells, maintenance closets, elevator shafts, pipe chases, mechanical rooms, duct shafts, bathrooms, and electrical closets. It can help to distribute these spaces onto the floors, but at the cost of long-term flexibility.

Psychological Functions

❑ *Orientation and transition.* Stepping through a door from the outside is a powerful sensory experience (figure 5.4). No one likes to be disoriented, and a vestibule, short hallway, or interior window can ready people for a change. Some entrances are meant to be dramatic: a theater, a museum, or a cathedral. Other entrances are stressful: to an operating room, a courtroom, or the boss' office. One creative example is a pediatric dentistry which provided enough space to transform its reception area into a miniature movie theater to distract the nervous patients and parents.

Figure 5.4 Church entry

❑ *Space as luxury.* Americans' need for space is much greater than every other culture's, but no matter what country, excess space is always a luxury. Should there be any luxurious space in the building? Where? In the entry or the executive suite? In the lunchroom? How much extra space is too much? The leader risks a permanent statement of selfishness if too much personal space is allotted to him or her.

❑ *Cultural expectations.* The floor plan should complement the organization's culture, whether formal or informal. One excellent book, *A Pattern Language: Towns, Buildings, Construction*, tells how in Peru there is a strict cultural prescription for how far guests can enter a home: new acquaintances only see the front parlor, while some friends may enter the dining room. Only close friends and family may advance to the kitchen.

❑ *Informal socialization.* The need for informal socialization is strong, and every building

Figure 5.5 Commerzbank cafeteria

must have loosely defined spaces: a break room, the student union, the doctor's lounge, and the stools in a bar (figure 5.5). People always gather around the food, the friendliest space in a home.

❑ *First and last impressions.* All leaders know the power of first impressions, whether their organization sells wrenches, high fashion, healthcare, or a government service. A powerful planning technique is to trace the tour the leader gives to prospective customers or staff. The script of that tour ("Here's a display," "Here's where we work," "Here's where we socialize") is a way to arrange one's thoughts about entries, corridors, and all the rooms.

Analyses and Observations

The initial floor plans must not by themselves set the shape of the building. In the next sections, "Siting, landscape, and nature" and "Exterior massing and interior volumes," we discuss how practical and psychological functions combine and conflict to produce a building's three-dimensional basic shape.

A well laid-out building is a pleasure to be in. A visitor feels comfortable even though all the uses cannot be seen from every room. Some people are better at spatial analysis than others, but pie charts of all space types—corridors, public spaces, private spaces, and support areas—can show if these spaces and experiences balance. One can also overlay the circulation arrows on the floor plan to visualize transitions and distances. A floor plan, like all architectural drawings, is a two-dimensional abstraction of a three-dimensional reality.

Architecture's complexity is too great to be resolved using only logic. The leader depends on the architect's creativity to produce a design that fulfills all the defined needs.

Element 2 • Siting, Landscaping, and Nature

Siting (how a building is placed on the land) and *landscaping* (how the land is altered to suit the building) clearly make up one element of architecture. The practical and psychological functions of both tap the energy of nature. All buildings, even the most mundane in the densest urban setting, are statements of how humans fit into their environment.

Figure 5.6 Rockefeller Plaza

Sometimes the project begins with laying out a campus of buildings, for which there are six rules:

1. Clearly identifiable entries: Staff and newcomers alike should be certain about where to enter the building.

2. Well-placed buildings with an obvious center: A tower or large courtyard will help everyone stay oriented and mentally connected to the campus.

3. Obvious building "edges": A wall should not block one's line of sight, but guide it helpfully toward an entry, exit, or feature.

4. Consistency or hierarchy of image: Stanford and Cambridge universities have very consistent architecture, adding to their sense of importance and place.

5. Organized circulation: Both pedestrian and vehicular circulation should be easy and obvious. We will discuss later the importance of wayfinding and the psychology of staying oriented.

6. Balance of buildings and public spaces: Too little greenspace prevents visitors and staff from understanding, much less appreciating, an otherwise well-designed building.

Landscaping is more than trees, plants, and ponds. Brick patios, outdoor lights, flag poles, parking lots, signs, and fountains make the land useful and inspiring (figure 5.6, above). Suburban and urban settings obviously differ. Some city buildings are nowhere near green space, but Foster and Partners' Commerzbank in Frankfurt has four-story gardens (figure 5.7) spiraling around the building's 53 floors.

The spiritual relationship of humans and nature is too deep to know fully. The buildings we build both defy and accept nature. Why do we need sunlight? Why do we love to hear water? Other than as safe shelter, are buildings ever better than nature?

Figure 5.7 Commerzbank garden

Figure 5.8 Machu Picchu in Peru

Practical Functions

❑ *Sunlight.* Clergyman and historian Thomas Fuller (1606–1661) said, "Light, God's elder daughter, is the principal beauty of a building." No matter how dramatic the building's facade or elaborate the artificial lights, the sun gives life to a building. Deciding how the building faces the morning and afternoon sun in spring and winter is literally of vital importance.

❑ *Regulations.* Communities heavily regulate how buildings use land. Zoning laws dictate green space borders (setbacks), the amount of parking, the width of drive aisles, the need for sidewalks, the intensity of landscaping, site grading for rain run-off, signage restrictions, exterior lighting requirements, and even the protection of the neighbor's view and sunshine. Many municipalities in America have a scoring system to ensure sufficient, even attractive landscaping. European nations have even stricter controls.

❑ *Topography and drainage.* The slope of a site radically affects the placement and shape of a building (figure 5.8). Rain run-off must be managed and melted snow must be kept from refreezing in dangerous places. Pedestrians and drivers should not be too challenged by the grades.

❑ *Site wayfinding and efficient entry.* The limitations on siting can conspire against putting the front door in the best place. Staff, as well as first-time visitors, should be certain about how to enter a building even when they are hundreds of feet away. The architect blends signs, sidewalks, and site lighting to complement the building and connect politely to the neighbors. A perfect design does not compromise among lesser evils, but creatively mixes the best ideas.

❑ *Regulating the wind.* Buildings can block or encourage the wind. Roman villas were designed with an open courtyard which allowed the sun and wind to enter during the right seasons and times of day and offered shelter when the sun and wind were too strong. As the Roman Empire spread, these designs were modified with taller walls or different rooflines to fit to the climate.

❏ *Parking and pedestrian circulation.* Parking lots and sidewalks are regulated in detail, and only a few parking patterns work well on any one site. Considerations are aisle widths, straight or angled parking stalls, turning radii, handicapped parking requirements, truck apron depths, and utility easements.

❏ *Soil conditions.* Building on poor soil is expensive, and the leader should conduct a geotechnical study before imagining a grand building—and closing on the lot. Manhattan is a pile of rock and an easy place to build. Boston is a sea of sloppy soils.

❏ *Expansion paths.* The architect must site the first phase of a building in anticipation of *all* the phases. That a building might need to grow in different directions adds to the complexity of the task. The leader should generally proclaim a clear confidence in the future, but might want quietly to encourage the facility planning team to maximize flexibility.

Psychological Functions

❏ *Welcoming approach and entry.* The transition from outside to inside must be thoughtfully paced. It is one thing to get people to your door; it is another to welcome them. The leader should imagine the visitor approaching the building in a car or by foot, walking closer to the building, and reaching for the door handle.

❏ *Relationship to nature.* Our environment may be harsh at times and often dramatically different in each season. A pleasant courtyard can protect people from sun, wind, and sounds, and provide a respite. In Chapter 5, we see how Thomas Jefferson's Monticello (figure 5.9) is as much about nature as it is about indoor spaces.

Figure 5.9 Monticello set in nature

❏ *Healing gardens.* More hospitals are creating "healing gardens" of different designs for children, the elderly, Alzheimer patients, and families. Many businesses never consider a garden, but even a tiny one, properly placed, offers relief and inspiration.

❏ *Relationship to one's neighbors.* Our social relationships are shaped by our buildings and vice versa. People raised in high-rise apartment buildings are different from people raised in farmhouses. Views of and distances to our neighbors affect us strongly.

A powerful example of siting is the United States Capitol, which sits on The Hill and visually aligns with the Washington Monument, the Lincoln Memorial and now the World War II Memorial.

Analyses and Observations

The first tool of site analysis is a two-dimensional plan. Aerial photographs of the site, its neighbors, and the community can provide a useful point of view, too. One can also have made a site model that shows the topography, trees, neighboring buildings, and eventually, the building itself (discussed in the next section on *massing*). There is no substitute for walking the site at different times of day, using corner stakes to visualize the building's position.

Figure 5.10 Guggenheim Museum

Frank Gehry's Guggenheim Museum in Bilbao, Spain (figure 5.10) is applauded as much for its siting as for its shape. A cottage sited nicely at the foot of an inland lake is just as successful as a suburban office building that is approachable and careful in how it uses the land.

Element 3 • Exterior Massing and Interior Volumes

Massing means the building's basic exterior shapes and proportions. Frank Lloyd Wright spoke of how the geometric blocks he played with as a child became the intellectual building blocks of his designs. Architects often build massing models early in their work. These models are usually made of wood, Styrofoam, or cardboard, and depict the building and how it relates to its neighbors. With good massing, the building will always feel right.

It is an ancient puzzle why humans feel better in buildings of certain *proportions,* the way the sizes of a design's elements relate to one another. The Greeks identified a proportion called the Golden Section or Golden Mean (approximately 1:1.62) that is found in the Parthenon and throughout architecture (figure 5.11). Other buildings are built to geometric proportions such as 1:1, 1:2, and 1:3. Le Corbusier, the famous Swiss architect of the early 20th century invented another satisfying system of proportion, Le Modular (figure 5.12), based on the proportions of the human body. Why does this system work? Which one is right for a particular community or market? Leaders do not need to know why humans respond to certain shapes: it is enough to see that one's architect has mastered proportion.

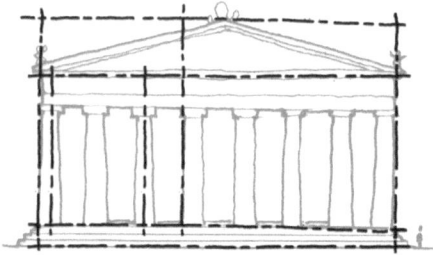
Figure 5.11 The Golden Section

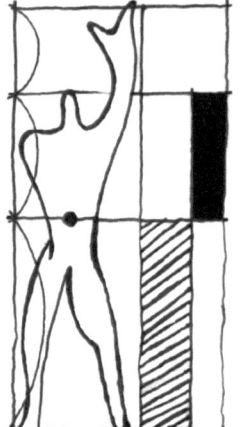
Figure 5.12 Le Modular

Interior volumes are the three-dimensional spaces inside the building, like invisible sculptures of air in which one can walk. Many offices are boring stacks and rows of rectangular blocks. But a cathedral's nave, the tent of an attic, or the sloped ceilings of a performance hall excite feelings of motion. Some volumes are purposely lower and narrower, such as a reading nook or a confessional. The volume under the United States Capitol's dome creates feelings of freedom and ambition—the sky is the limit. But above all, people crave variety.

Scale is the bigness or smallness of something compared to its surroundings, and it is essential to getting the interior volumes right. Should the building have a human scale to make people comfortable, or should it be monumental to convey an idea larger than life?

Figure 5.13 Guggenheim entry

Like proportion and scale, *symmetry* is another basic design principle. Why is symmetry so comforting? Some architects design powerfully asymmetrical or amorphous shapes (Gehry's Bilbao museum, for example, figure 5.13). They usually trace these designs to forms from nature—suggesting the ultimate source of all successful design.

Practical Functions

❑ *Enclosing the floor plans.* The *footprint*, the ground level floor plan of the building, can be the shape of the most efficient floor plan, but choosing a shape is rarely that simple. We explore below the practical and psychological forces that push and tug at the building's basic mass. A football stadium must fit its "floor plan," but other large buildings work well as a square or rectangle or shaped like an **L**, a **U**, or an **O**.

❑ *Cost control.* Simple shapes are less expensive to build, but the site might not permit it. While the square footage might fit better on one large floor, the site might force the building into two smaller floors with a basement. Tall buildings often cost most per square foot than short ones: the need for elevators, the space lost to stairs, and the expense of a sturdier structure affect the budget and, therefore, decisions about the building's shape.

Figure 5.14 Generic architecture

❑ *Adapting to climate.* In Iceland, roofs are not only steeply pitched, but tilted to blunt the wind and shed the snow. In hot climates, buildings might enclose a courtyard to provide shade or collect the breeze. Large eaves can serve the same purpose. Americans depend too much on technology to combat the elements, and generic-looking buildings are the sad result. A building whose shape ignores climate will never look or feel like it belongs on its site. (figure 5.14).

❑ *Views and sightlines.* The shape of the building should make the point of entry obvious and guide the eye as the visitor approaches and enters the site. In "Element 2: Siting, Landscaping, and Nature," we discuss how a building's orientation affects sightlines to and from the building; distant views from a tall building are very different from views from the first story. Security is improved, too, when corners and doors are easy to see.

The height, breadth, and orientation of a large wall are opportunities to admit natural light.

❑ *Energy use.* Large interior volumes demand more energy to heat and cool. Some huge spaces are dramatic, but mechanical engineers then need to compensate to meet the user's primary need for comfortable temperatures and airflow.

❑ *Structure, systems, and zoning.* New York City's fabulous stepped-back skyscrapers result from zoning laws written to prevent streets from becoming shadow canyons. *Floor area ratios* (the ratio of a building's square footage to its site) are a common zoning tool to restrict size and height. The structural system limits building shape, too: some forms possible in steel cannot be built in concrete or wood. But exotic technologies are not needed to make interesting shapes. Chicago architect Joe Valerio has shaped building envelopes by tilting large concrete panels, such as on his 3COM building (figure 5.15) near Chicago; he also designed an inflatable band shell.

Figure 5.15 3COM campus

Psychological Functions

❑ *Staying oriented with edges.* A building's outside walls form the edges of two shapes: the shape of the building inside the walls and the shape of the spaces outside the building. Architects employ building edges to guide people to and around the building; this makes the building sensible and friendly. On a building's perimeter, arcades and courtyards help visitors make a transition into and out of nature.

❑ *Scaled to impress.* Grandeur and modesty are both tools of leadership. Osaka Castle (figure 5.16) is awe inspiring, particularly when it was built in 1615. Shogun Tokugawa Ieyasu's point was plain: "I am supremely powerful." The low door of a Japanese teahouse makes the opposite point: shogun and peasant alike must humble themselves when entering.

Figure 5.16 Osaka Castle

Design: Practical and Psychological Functionality 73

Figure 5.17 Fallingwater

Figure 5.18 Service garage

- *Anticipate what is inside.* The building's massing should suggest to people who are approaching what the spaces inside might be like. It is comforting to say to oneself, "That low part is obviously the entry; there's the waiting room, and that's obviously the cafeteria. There are the patient towers."

- *Harmony with nature.* Osaka Castle exemplifies a design fitted to its natural setting, "a cascade of roofs," as architect and writer Christopher Alexander describes it. Frank Lloyd Wright said that "no house should be on a hill or in a hill, but *of* a hill," a matter of siting and scale and proportion. His Fallingwater is an obvious example (figure 5.17).

Analyses and Observations

Cultural preferences are powerful determinants of a building's shape. Americans expect a barn to have its gambrel shape, a house to sport a triangular dormer, and a bungalow to wear a front porch. These shapes have strong associations from our upbringings: we can deviate, of course, but only with care.

The careful leader revisits the site, perhaps with the massing model on a table and tries hard to imagine the scale and proportions of the completed structure.

Practical-minded executives often struggle with aesthetic decisions. However, experience and instinct teach us not to ignore an issue just because we cannot understand it logically.

Madison Gas & Electric Company needed a new service garage, and anticipated building a purely functional box of a building. But after considering the psychological implications of its company culture and the needs of the community, it invested successfully in something more interesting (figure 5.18).

Element 4 • Structural Materials and Colors

What should a building be made of? Even when the choices of materials were limited, practical and psychological functions led to startling solutions: the Parthenon could have been built of wood, but Athena might have been displeased. The plaster ceiling of the Notre Dame is cut and painted to resemble stone blocks. Today, even modest buildings are composites of exotic materials such as structural glass, titanium, engineered wood laminate, and fiberglass.

A basic design question is whether the exterior building material one sees should be what the building is actually made of. The first skyscrapers were like Chicago's Monadnock Building (1891), an all-masonry building whose ground floor walls are six feet thick to support the weight of the walls above. Only a few blocks away is its structural descendent, the Reliance Building (1894), built of a steel frame with a masonry skin. While of similar height, the revolutionary lightweight structure of the Reliance Building allowed it to have large windows. Some would say the Monadnock Building is aesthetically more "honest" than the Reliance Building's "superficial" skin.

A Southwestern adobe house shows another choice of structure and color, using local materials that reflect the community's roots in the landscape. The oldest farmhouses of the Midwest are built of wood from nearby forests. Modern transport and manufacturing skills make most materials available everywhere.

Figure 5.19 John Hancock building

The John Hancock building in Chicago (figure 5.19) reveals its structural design and its structural materials; one can plainly see the overlap of architecture and engineering. The building is black to emphasize its monumentality. Conversely, a group of 20th century American architects was called The Whites: the absence of color was meant to convey an honesty of structure (figure 5.20).

Figure 5.20 Getty Museum

Practical Functions

❑ *Strength against weight.* A building must hold itself up; it has to withstand the pull of gravity, the push of storms, the weight of snow and people and their gear, as well as the forces of earthquakes and settling soils. Buildings move: the Hancock Building's 100 floors sway two feet in a strong wind, and large buildings have expansion joints for the shrinking and swelling caused by cold and heat. A smart leader respects the structural engineers and their world of live loads, dead loads, and tension, torque, and compression.

❑ *Protection against the elements.* A building must keep out rain and drafts, and protect its inhabitants from fire, floods, intense sounds, and harsh sunlight. Structural materials are insulators and regulators: adobe releases heat in the cool evenings, and the open arches of a Turkish courtyard let the breezes blow through. Buildings have used natural and artificial insulators of all kinds: snow blocks, hollow bricks, fiberglass, Styrofoam, and dirt. We discuss energy conservation on page 101.

❑ *Opening up interior spaces and views.* A column-free interior is costly and limits the structural options, but stadiums, factories, and churches run better without columns in the way. A column-free interior also offers more opportunities for interior arrangement of elements. The structural function of the Houston Astrodome is obviously different from that of an igloo or a gas station.

❑ *Availability and speed of construction.* A steel igloo would show a poor choice of structural materials. Modern builders can choose among steel (and steel cables), stone, masonry, concrete, wood, and glass, depending on the economy, weather, and the skills of local craftspeople. Large contractors have the equipment, staff, and techniques to expand the options.

Figure 5.21 Tower of Pisa

❑ *Regulations and covenants.* Some communities or developers limit the materials from which a building can be built. These rules are usually a reasonable backstop to poor quality.

❑ *Geo-technical considerations.* Geo-technical engineers consider the strength and stability of the soils, as well as the action of the water table, and now, environmental liabilities. The town leaders of Pisa may have wished their tower had been built on a better site (figure 5.21).

❑ *Conservation and preservation.* Not all new projects are made with new materials: even bricks and concrete can be recycled. York Minster Cathedral was constructed on the site of a huge medieval church, which was built over a Roman fort, which was itself built over an ancient Celtic settlement. Some new buildings use ancient building technologies, such as rammed earth or hay bales, because of their local availability and eco-friendliness. There are drawbacks: while a practical argument can be made for a thatched roof, the rain of spiders may diminish its charm.

Psychological Functions

Technology and creativity allow limitless combinations of stone, metal, glass, bricks, and wood, each in a wide variety of sizes, shapes, colors, and textures. All these materials can support a building: to make the right choice, we need now to explore the idea of the psychology of structure.

❏ *Standard of quality.* It may be economical to build one's building of inexpensive wood framing and stucco (now a fiberglass paste), but even visitors who know nothing of construction will intuit this is an organization uninterested in quality.

❏ *Feelings of permanence and weight.* There was an era when all banks were built of granite to convey a sense of permanence and security. The grand buildings of Chicago's 1893 Colombian Exposition were built of light timbers covered with a mixture of straw and plaster. The result was the White City, temporary monuments of what was to be the neoclassical architecture of the future (an oxymoron, Wright was quick to say).

❏ *Figurative transparency.* A stone bank and a glass bank make very different impressions. If weight conveys permanence, transparency conveys honesty and welcome. Transparency is not just about windows, but how approaching guests and employees see deep into the building. Ludwig Mies van der Rohe, whose Crown Hall we study later, used stark simplicity of structure to open the connection between indoors and outdoors (figure 5.22).

Figure 5.22 Farnsworth House

❏ *Honest expression of structure.* Chicago's Reliance Building (designed by Burnham and Root) is a structure with a skeleton of one material and a skin of another. Much of the appeal of Frank Lloyd Wright's Prairie architecture is that both shapes and the materials are of the earth. There is nothing superficial. This integrity contrasts with the manipulative superficiality of a fast food restaurant: rooflines trick the eye and no honest structure is seen anywhere. These buildings do not want you to stay long.

❏ *Approachability.* A childcare center is built with bright colors and friendly textures to invite touch and play. The cool, white surfaces of the Taj Mahal are serene, not intimidating; the regular, off-white clapboards of a Quaker church welcomes its friends; the black, hard, and smooth surfaces of the Hancock Building make one feel one needs permission to enter.

Analyses and Observations

An igloo and the Hancock Building are architecturally similar in their uniformity of material and color. The black **V** of the granite Vietnam Veterans Memorial makes it a bold work of architecture of strong purpose. It is a mark of great talent to make such a design succeed: computer models cannot replace seeing and feeling large samples of the materials.

A leader cannot be afraid of complexity and contrast. The reward might be a beautiful combination of rough stone, raw steel, smooth glass, and rugged timbers. Successful simplicity and successful complexity are measures of a great building.

Element 5 · Windows, Light, and Rhythm

Windows have strangely different aspects. From the inside looking out, windows define the views and let light in. Seen from the outside, the pattern of the windows and doors creates a rhythm of shapes on the surface of the building. Large windows let our imaginations reach in and out of the building. The changing quality of light makes the building come alive: it connects everyone to the pulse of the day and seasons (figure 5.23).

Figure 5.23 Grand Central Station

There is an endless variety of windows types and configurations, an architectural choice called *fenestration*. Windows and doors are elements of the building's aesthetic composition, the artful arrangement of parts and subparts.

Practical Functions

❑ *Sunlight for work.* No argument is needed in favor of enough light, but a common problem is too much light. Natural light can create glare, shadows, and too much heat. An architect's client may demand, "Light, light, light!" and then draw the shades. Frosted or ribbed glass can provide both control and privacy. A test of a good design is how seldom blinds and drapes are closed.

❑ *Ventilation.* New window and mechanical technologies ventilate buildings more naturally than the generation of 20th century buildings that depended entirely on mechanical engineering for conditioning the air. Americans consume huge amounts of electricity to move heat from one place to another when operable windows would work more efficiently.

❑ *Merchandising.* A Christmas tradition in Chicago is strolling the wonderful mechanical displays in Marshall Field's store windows. But organizations other than stores can use glass walls, doors, and corridors to give visitors a glimpse of the interesting things being done inside. The Rose Center for Earth and Space in New York is an example (figure 5.24).

Figure 5.24 Rose Center at night

Psychological Functions

❏ *Views.* Why are views so important to people? To rest our eyes? To rest our minds? To stay in tune with the weather? To satisfy an instinct for an escape route? All humans enjoy the beauty of a landscape or a cityscape.

❏ *Security.* It takes careful thought to place exterior and interior windows that allow workers to look out, yet not feel spied upon by others looking in. No one likes to be watched while they work. This is a topic we pick up later when we discuss furniture.

❏ *American differences.* American workspaces, even for highly paid staff, often provide too little natural light. In contrast, German law mandates every worker be no more than so many meters from a window. As a result, German buildings have a great deal of glass and slender floor plans. Americans might call these buildings inefficient; others call them healthy. Some American's idea of space use efficiency results in lightless spaces that actually reduce productivity.

Analyses and Observations

The *elevation* is a basic architectural drawing, the perfect side view of the building (figure 5.25), showing the pattern of windows and doors. Most architectural drawings, like the one shown, are *orthogonal,* meaning they are drawn without perspective or foreshortening. The builders can use a scale to measure these drawings for construction purposes. Architectural renderings, in black and white or in color, are drawn in more life-like perspective for the benefit of the client and the designers. Three-dimensional models are invaluable for refining window and door placement. *Computer-aided drafting and design* (CADD) affords leaders an idea about how the color and materials of the windows, doors, frames, coverings, and hardware combine into a single, yet functional, artistic expression.

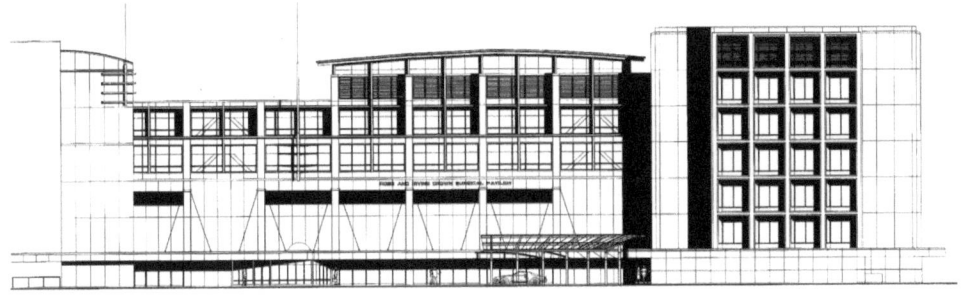

Figure 5.25 Architectural elevation

Element 6 ▪ Interior Colors and Textures

Colors serve practical functions, and their psychological effects are strong. They should align with and encourage the work being done, not militate silently against it. Colors change with the texture of their material: a plaster wall and a brick wall painted with the same yellow paint look different. The texture determines how color reflects light, and the tiny, even microscopic shadows change a color's appearance at different times of day.

People can favor different senses: vision, touch, hearing, smell, or taste. Like good food, textured surfaces stimulate several senses at once and, therefore, our imaginations. The textures of glass, brick, wood, grass, concrete, steel, and plastic that we see, hold, and walk on constantly affect our mood. A leader can give colors different meanings; advertising reminds us how color can manipulate facts and feelings. Complementary colors provide comfort; contrasts provide energy.

Practical Functions

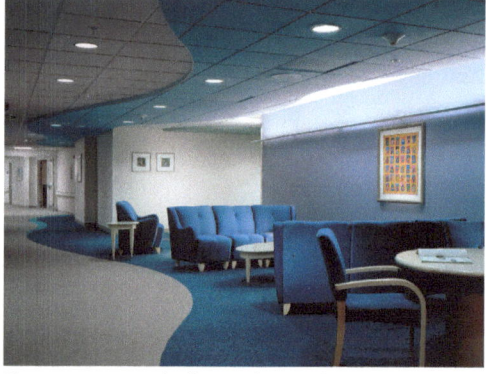

Figure 5.26 Wayfinding colors and textures

❑ *Wayfinding.* Hospitals use color to direct people: public corridors might have a yellow stripe; red thresholds mean "do not enter;" and banks of elevators can be color-coded to orient distracted patients (figure 5.26). Such obvious devices are necessary in our frantic world.

❑ *Temperature and glare control.* One can achieve passive cooling and heating by installing white flooring where the summer sun beats down and black stone floors where the winter sun angles in. Installing mis-sized and mis-placed windows can result in strong sunlight bouncing off glossy colors and smooth surfaces—generating glare and unwanted heat.

❑ *Identity.* Many organizations are identified with a color: the blue of the United Nations, the blue in the American flag, the blue of the IBM logo. Color can be loud, but subtlety is usually more effective. Adults can appreciate many shades of color and message.

❑ *Acoustic control.* Textures affect sound as well as color: hard, smooth surfaces like a basketball court can reflect, confuse, and amplify noise. As with light and color, a wise leader sets a clear objective for sound in every work area. The world is getting louder. Employees generally fare best when they can control the noise level of their surroundings. Should we begin to think about "acoustic health?"

Psychological Functions

❑ *Cultural references and fashion.* Culture and climate affect the local psychology of color. White is the funeral color in Buddhist countries. A Mediterranean sky tints a white building differently than does the harsh sun of the American southwest. Colors also have fashions: the 1960s had fluorescent and primary colors, the 1970s had a brief return to pastels, and the 1990s saw a retreat to blacks, whites, and grays. Individual color preferences are subjective, not logical; however, there is a science of color that one can use to advantage.

Figure 5.27 Monticello colors

❑ *Personal preferences.* A good leader does not choose colors based solely on personal preference, but selects colors that reflect the spirit of the organization. A leader should be at least a little bold in color choices, as was Thomas Jefferson at his Monticello (figure 5.27).

❑ *Intimacy.* The textures of what we touch in a building should be chosen with the same combination of science and intuition as the colors. Door handles, countertops, cafeteria trays, silverware, and bathroom fixtures can be cold or warm, rough or smooth. Wood grains, plaster, or stainless steel each set a specific tone.

❑ *Complement the furniture.* The design spirit in the building should be the same as that in the furniture. Both the building and its furniture lose if the colors and textures have neither a sensible nor sensitive connection.

Analyses and Observations

Interior colors should have some relationship to each other and the exterior. Passing through a door or hall should provide a seamless transition. Unless a dramatic effect is called for, one should choose complementary colors for the exterior and interior.

Choosing colors takes time. Some leaders find it easy while others never become comfortable with it. The architect should mock up large samples of the proposed textures and colors. One should see these samples in different lights, at different times of day, and remember the purpose of each color and texture.

Element 7 • Lighting, Ventilation, and Acoustics

Primitive buildings centered on the hearth for heat and light. Architecture is more than its physical space; it is also the atmosphere within and around it. Light, air and sound quality affect our relationship to the building. Hearing a Bach organ recital under Notre Dame's rose windows is an unforgettable experience.

Comfort is both practical and psychological. Healthy air, adequate lights for each task, and the right hum of activity energize employees to work more productively. Though men and women differ somewhat in this, a worker's second need (after natural light) is for comfortable heating and cooling. The executives who select building systems usually spend less time in their offices than anyone, so they need to observe first hand how employees interact with the environment. Needs vary by task and individual preferences. Though these systems are invisible, they drive productivity and, therefore, profit.

Like temperature and light, people respond to noise and smells differently and deeply. Some work best in silence, some in a busy shop. Others need both in alternation. Our world is loud, and quiet is a luxury.

Practical Functions

❑ *Good work.* Carpenters know that "good light makes good work," yet most workplaces are poorly lighted. Weather and season affect the amount of available indoor light (figure 5.28). Light for tasks, light for mood, light for health, light for accent—all are important.

❑ *Safety.* Making safety a priority is a proven act of leadership, and light means

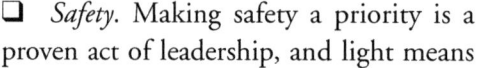

Figure 5.28 Lighting for good work

safety, particularly in parking lots and public spaces. Regulations require lighted exit signs, flashing lights for the deaf, emergency sirens for the blind, emergency ventilation for smoke exhaust, sprinklers for fire, and venting for noxious fumes.

❑ *Health.* The mills of the Industrial Revolution were among the most vicious buildings ever erected: deafening and dim, children were blinded, and the fumes killed people outright. Every leader must soberly assess the harm their building can inflict; negligence can degrade the health and morale of their entire workforce. Cities are still poisonous places, and a leader should direct the architect to create an environment that is healing.

❑ *Advertising.* The smell of garlic, lighted product displays, and piped in music promote sales in restaurants, stores, and sports stadiums. A good salesperson never passes an opportunity to set the stage for his or her products. It is instructive to study the

Design: Practical and Psychological Functionality 83

Figure 5.29 Retail lighting types

many *kinds* of lighting in a Starbucks (figure 5.29).

Psychological Functions

❏ *Coaxing nature inside.* Safe experiences in nature are mentally healthy. This is why we always need the lights, sounds, and smells—the forces—of nature. Small buildings with operable windows in rural settings make this easy, but big buildings with vast interior spaces compel the architect to fake nature: colored lamps, water fountains, humidified air, and music or white noise. But, interior landscaping is the best way to evoke the outdoors.

❏ *Offering comfort.* No patient wants mysterious lighting anywhere in a hospital. Clean, warm light reduces uncertainty. Like many other buildings, a hospital needs private and social areas that are restful changes in atmosphere from the anxiety of the treatment rooms. Level of brightness directly affects perceptions.

❏ *Drama and mood.* Lighting and sound play a role in the psychology of leadership. The artful use of darkness, as in a theater, restaurant, or coffee shop, speaks to the skill and courage of the architect. Dramatic or subtle lighting and hushed or bright acoustics can be backdrop to the leader's story.

Analyses and Observations

Though some projects need specialized lighting, designers and acoustical engineers, many buildings suffer simply because the leader did not insist on a discussion of light, sound, and air. Leaders should ask about the color, intensity, control, and direction of the light in each room: Will everyone have the light they need to do good work, but not strain their eyes? What will staff hear in this room? Should the ventilation be special? Will the atmosphere give them healthy energy? Lighting and acoustic controls are necessities, not a psychological flourish.

Wisconsin's State Capitol, designed in 1913 by George Post, has no direct light: the windows, light fixtures, and skylights are all of frosted glass (figure 5.30). The result is there are no shadows and everything can be seen evenly—the perfect message for the people's political house.

Figure 5.30 Wisconsin State Capitol

Element 8 ▪ Furniture

Like a building, furniture is concerned with massing, materials, color, textures, mechanics, and of course, ergonomics. Furniture plays a role in psychological functions as well. The quality of American furniture construction is high and that quality itself is a great psychological benefit in reinforcing a message of stability and quality.

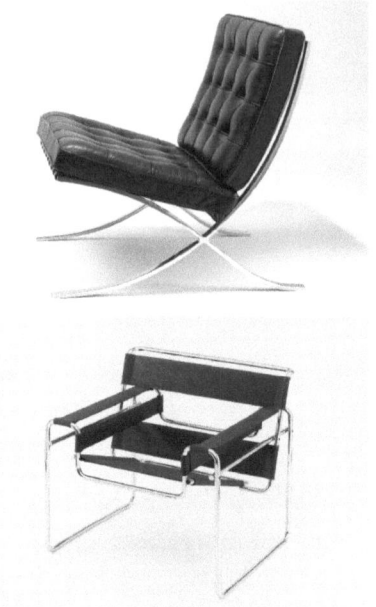

Architects often design furniture. Two of the architects reviewed earlier, Walter Gropius and Mies van der Rohe, designed chairs that are both now museum pieces *and* still in use (figures 5.31 and 5.32). It is simple sense to ask the architect of the building to at least participate in the furniture selection.

In *The Ten Pillars of Architecture*, the Roman architect Vitruvius wrote that every building should have *integritas;* that is, each element

Figures 5.31 Chair by Walter Gropius and 5.32 Chair by Mies van der Rohe

should be seen and felt to be of a whole, whether as a complement or sensible contrast. Things can have *integritas* without being identical. A set of six perfectly matched chairs has *integritas,* but in a safe and unimaginative way. Six chairs of the same design but in six shades of pink have a more interesting integrity, but perhaps not in the White House. Six completely mismatched chairs may, however, fit perfectly in a college frat house. Every building creates its own context and each element must fit in its own way.

Practical Functions

❑ *Work of all kinds.* The practical functions of furniture are obvious, whether freestanding or built in, custom or stock. What good is an efficient building with inefficient furniture? Furniture can be too small or too big for a job; it can be too high or too low; it can have too few drawers or shelves. The wrong furniture wastes hundreds of small movements a day; it creates clutter and so reduces concentration. It is easy to lose 5 percent in productivity because the furniture—whether an executive desk or a warehouse packing table—is wrong.

❑ *Material handling and storage.* Furniture and cabinets are tools in every organization's work: why not give everyone the right tool for each job? Copy room cabinets, warehouse racking, medical records storage, library shelves, and retail displays are kinds of furniture. Science and creativity can address these practical problems. For example, a clothing retailer put a bowl of unshelled peanuts at the front door and the customers were told that they could drop the shells on the floor. At the end of the day, the trails and piles of shells revealed which racks were positioned best.

❑ *Health and trash.* Executives may not be aware how much space and equipment it takes to keep a building clean and safe. In maintenance closets, shops, and docks one finds shelves, sinks, bins, toolboxes, lockers, compactors, carts, broom hooks, hose reels, first aid stations, fire extinguishers, and trash and recycling containers. Kitchens have a waste removal process of their own. An attentive leader takes time to consider these functions.

❑ *Flexible connections.* The right furniture with generous data connections allows the organization to adapt. While some people work well with clutter, most do not: well-placed outlets and task lighting allow individuals to adjust their workspace. Technologies are changing rapidly, so this requires hard analysis of how best to accommodate predictable and unpredictable changes.

Dilbert lives! System furniture dealers promise greater productivity, teamwork, and flexibility, but the truth is that almost everyone hates cubicles. They do not automatically make people more productive or team spirited: they are a necessary space-saving evil.

Psychological Functions

❑ *Intimacy and privacy.* Most staff spend all day at their desk or station, and so its comforts mean more to them than to leaders, who travel often. A few inches of height in someone's work surface, chair, or the dividers among neighboring workstations can make a radical difference in attitude.

❑ *Personalization.* Given the intimacy of a workspace, staff should be able to personalize their work area at least a little. A policy both allowing and limiting personalization is wise. It is interesting that Winston Churchill and Thomas Jefferson used a similar style of standup desk.

Figure 5.33 FDR in the Oval Office, 1935

❑ *Status.* A large desk of high quality is a powerful status symbol (figure 5.33); we remember that Franklin D. Roosevelt understood the power of design when commissioning the Pentagon. Even the most humble leader must decide how his or her workplace can promote a useful sense of order and authority: otherwise, the status-seeking in office furnishings can become brutal.

❑ *Socialization.* The success of a meeting can hinge on the shape of its table. Round tables such as King Arthur's promote discussion; oval or rectangular tables promote presentation. A long table with benches creates family-style informality, but a long table with twelve leather seats creates a dozen points of view. The room must fit the furniture and vice versa, a reminder that the elements of architecture must be developed simultaneously.

Analyses and Observations

The leader might be shocked to hear what the staff really feel about their furniture. Before buying 1,000 desks or workstations, the leader should buy one and encourage people to see it, touch it, and use it, ideally near the sample colors and materials of the new building.

Element 9 ▪ Details, Decoration, and Art

Figure 5.34 Notre Dame

There are three kinds of exterior and interior architectural details. The first kind is purely technical and often unseen, such as the welding specifications for structural steel. The second kind of detail is purely decorative or symbolic (figure 5.34), such as crown molding or the grout pattern in a tile floor. The third kind is both necessary and decorative, such as a door handle: even the plainest makes a statement. The mullions in a cottage window, the wrought iron railings on New Orleans's Bourbon Street, Tiffany lamps, the spindles in a Victorian staircase, and the brickwork of a Prairie Style fireplace are examples of the third type.

Why decorate? Why pay for crown molding or tile insets or gargoyles? Some architects oppose pure decoration. They believe that the true spirit of the building emerges if *only* the practical functions are considered.

Visible details, such as one's clothes, make a statement no matter how indifferent the leader might be. Every building has hundreds of details and, like the details in a good novel, they bring the building to life, hold it together, and tell a story. Being small, details work subtly: if the light fixtures, door handles, sign brackets, and window frames have sharp edges in chrome, the building has a different feel than if they have rounded edges in brass. Inconsistent details are disorienting; getting them right is hard, worthwhile work.

Churches, schools, and government buildings often display art, and the building should highlight these messages. The Sistine Chapel in the Vatican is an obvious example. Few businesses have meaningful artwork to display, playing it safe with prints of ducks. Better to purchase a few professionally chosen and placed artworks that are in sync with one's mission.

Practical Functions

❑ *Construction quality.* Most details prescribe how a building is built, and thereby, define its quality. Girder connections, wall and window frames, air conditioning ductwork and controls, elevator equipment, site utility connections, and so on need to be detailed skillfully and thoroughly to produce quality construction.

❑ *Maintenance.* A roof with the wrong flashing or gutters will rot and then leak. This idea reaches into every corner of the building: how the tile is set, floor joints are caulked, landscaping watered, toilets mounted, ceilings hung. While a leader need not be concerned with every item, he or she must set a standard of performance in the facility plan that the architect and engineers can make real in the details.

❑ *Weatherization.* Different climates demand different weather-related details. Joints, walls, floors, and windows must be flexible for New York's 100 degree temperature changes. Tolerances can be smaller in more temperate zones. The details of insulation, frost protection, humidity, and pest control all need to be considered.

❑ *Signage.* Buildings can wear hundreds of signs, on the site, in the parking lot, at the main entry, by each suite, for the restrooms. Signs identify, direct, inform, remind, caution, and advertise. Words, logos, arrows, and other symbols engage the mind at a subconscious level. Consider how all the signs in a large airport affect one's experience by their materials, colors, placement, and lighting.

❑ *Advertising and display.* Every organization has products or artifacts to display. For a manufacturer, the product display case is perhaps the most overt and important message the building sends. Display walls, visitor centers, or viewing corridors should be part of the design concept from the beginning. Architecture does not always have to be subtle.

Psychological Functions

❑ *Integration.* Details add continuity from room to room if they share a complementary palette of materials, colors, textures, and shapes. The building gains integrity if the door handles, light fixtures, and handrails are of a family. Using variations of one carpet pattern can have the same effect. Too much similarity leaves the design boring, but too little is disorienting and "off message."

❑ *Cultural ties.* Some details were so widely used in the past that they become a cultural signature (figure 5.35), making it

Figure 5.35 American Gothic (detail)

difficult to try something new. Examples are the scrollwork on a Swiss chalet and the classic triangular entablature over a bank entrance.

❑ *Links to nature.* All the elements of architecture can link healthfully to nature, and the details of planters, interior paving, and fountains can conjure the natural details of life, as well as soften the environment.

❑ *Fun and surprise.* Large buildings can be overwhelming, but playful touches carefully placed can keep everyone energized. Dining areas are good spots for fun: movie posters, fanciful light fixtures, unconventional furniture, and unlikely wall shapes can be stimulating changes from more serious parts of the building.

Analyses and Observations

A good way to evaluate an architect's attitudes, skill, and experience is by touring their buildings with an eye to the details. A building may be impressive in its massing and major materials, but, as in anything, it is attention to detail that reveals commitment to quality. As Mies van der Rohe proclaimed, "God is in the details!"

Six Instructive Buildings

In our discussion of the nine elements of architecture, we uncovered several themes: the links of architecture to nature and to human nature, the connections between physical comfort and mental energy, the creative use of construction technologies, the intensity of regulations, the variety of ethical considerations, the effects of culture and of climate, the growing need for security, and the roles of light and color outside and in.

There are infinite design solutions to fulfill the almost 90 practical and psychological functions outlined earlier. In this section we meet six architects with strong—and strongly differing—ideas about functions and forms and about how those ideas play out in their masterpieces.

Monticello (1768)

Figure 5.36 Monticello approach

Thomas Jefferson's Monticello in Virginia (figure 5.36) was started in 1768, and he redesigned and renovated it throughout his lifetime. His retreat from the "hated occupation of politics," he used Monticello to entertain, study, manage his plantation (and slaves), conduct experiments, and to be alone with his family. Jefferson was famously independent, opinionated, and extravagant—but also a man of limitless curiosity and inventiveness, and his home reflects his character. Jefferson loved things European and studied the Italian Renaissance architect Andrea Palladio (1508–80), himself a student of ancient Roman "taste, genius, and magnificence." Jefferson berated the buildings around him as "billboards of colonial dependence." While Monticello is not of course modern architecture, it is arguably the most American building and the kind of neoclassical design many 20th century architects wanted to reinvent.

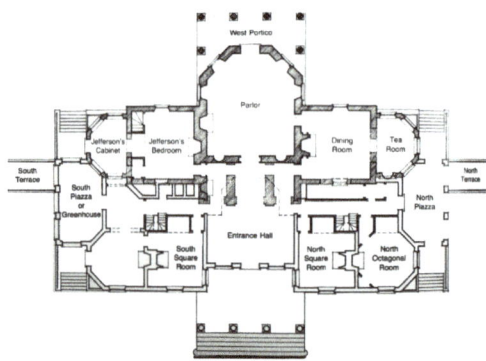
Figure 5.37 Monticello floor plan

The floor plan (figure 5.37) shows the mix of rooms, some encouraging flow from one to the other, some creating distance and privacy. The entrance hall, the dining room, and the parlor are rooms for entertaining. Then there is Jefferson's remote *sancto sanctorum*, his study and bedroom. The transitions, or spaces between spaces, regulate the degree of privacy.

Monticello means little mountain, and the building is sited at the high point of 5,000 acres. There are both formal gardens (all of Jefferson's design) and a well-tended forest as well as greenhouses and vegetable gardens. Plants that Lewis and Clark brought back from their western odyssey still thrive today. The connections to nature are obvious in every direction.

The massing of the building shows straightforward classical symmetry and familiar proportions. The allusions to ancient Rome and Greece are obvious, yet with Jeffersonian—American—variations: it was scaled to be a private home, not a palace. The bricks and wood and white paint were all local materials and have become a palette used hundreds of thousands of times across the country. Jefferson was the inventor of the double-hung window whose placement sets the rhythm of the exterior design and allowed the scientist-president the light he needed for study.

The interior colors are bold: blue, green, violet, and yellow give each room a theme (figure 5.38). The plaster walls, wood floors, wallpaper from Paris, and the interior dome made each room uniquely suited to its function and mood. The candlelight, fireplaces, and the feel and smell of the clean air must have stimulated intimate conversation. Then there was a bell system of Jefferson's invention to communicate throughout the house and service buildings.

Figure 5.38 Monticello fireplace

Jefferson designed much of the furniture to fit his particular needs: the dining table could be disassembled to clear the room for recitals. His bed was lodged between his study and library and open to both sides. His inventive details are famous: dumbwaiters, a clock that marks the seasons, a revolving clothes rack at the foot of his bed, and on and on. Monticello was a museum even in Jefferson's time; he collected the best of American art with the explicit purpose of preserving and promoting America's new culture.

Bauhaus (1926)

Figure 5.39

Walter Gropius (1883–1969), the son of an architect, studied architecture in Munich and Berlin, and entered private practice in 1910. He was a decorated cavalry lieutenant in World War I, but like other artists, felt that the horrors of war called for new ways of thinking about the world. The building in figure 5.39 is the 1926 Bauhaus school in Dessau, Germany. The school was not only for architecture, but also for new art forms and industrial designs that could be mass-produced and shared widely in society. This building, like all the others presented here, may not seem radical now, but showcased entirely new ideas when it was built. Before leaving for America in 1934, Gropius faced down the Gestapo to defend his untraditional ideas.

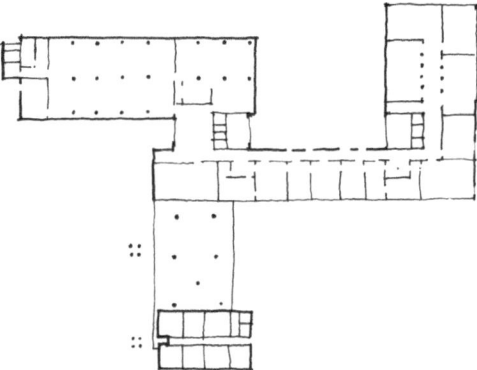

Figure 5.40 Bauhaus floor plan

New structural construction technologies allowed an open floor plan that had never been seen before; interior supporting walls were no longer needed. The school included classrooms, a lecture theater, workshops, a dining hall, and offices. Organized around a central axis, the floor plan (figure 5.40) unified architectural components that have, in Gropius' words, the "salutary effect of imparting that homogeneous character... which is the distinguishing mark of a superior worker culture." This was the primary psychological function the architect wanted to achieve.

Figure 5.41 Bauhaus Building auditorium

Gropius wanted a simple, direct connection to nature and the building sits "lightly, yet firmly upon the face of the earth." The courtyards encouraged the students to mingle and connect to the local social fabric. The flat roof—another innovation made possible by steel and concrete technologies—created an unusual cubist massing: the building invites people to see it in new ways from all sides. The huge glass walls create a forceful openness, with the purpose of providing everyone a healthy work environment (figure 5.41).

The glass walls also allow natural light to paint the interior. Unlike Monticello, the interior colors are a neutral backdrop to the activities inside. The varieties of textures—glass, wood, plaster, concrete, steel—would then have seemed intense, but were suited to the radical intellectualism of the Bauhaus movement.

The Bauhaus movement also turned its attention to crafts and furniture (figure 5.42). Its underlying philosophy was that mass-produced crafts are more honest, fitting to the age, and egalitarian. (The architect Michael Graves makes the same point today with his line of products sold through Target department stores.) The building deliberately has no historical detailing: the Bauhaus movement equated crown molding to the crowns of the elite.

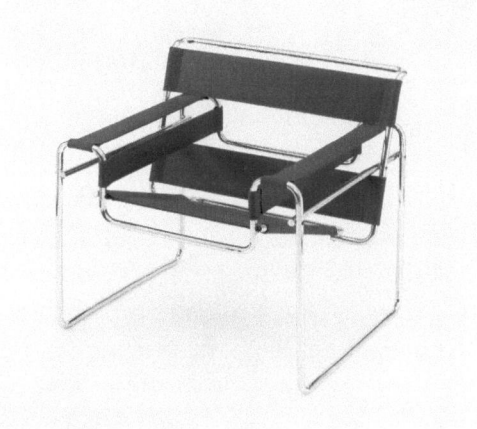

Figure 5.42 Chair by Walter Gropius

Johnson Wax Building (1939)

Figure 5.43 Johnson Wax Research Tower

Frank Lloyd Wright (1867–1959), who liked few people, liked the European architects least of all. He once remarked, when Gropius introduced himself, "Herr Gropius, welcome to America. I must be going," and commanded his chauffeur to drive off. He felt European buildings were too logical, too much alike, and too disconnected from nature. Wright was nearly as disdainful of his clients' ideas and money. But he was a genius, an innovator, an engineer, and among America's great artists. He designed hundreds of buildings in his long career: houses, office towers, stores, the Imperial Hotel in Japan (one of the few large buildings to survive the 1923 Tokyo earthquake), government buildings, churches, and on and on. One of his largest and most complex projects was the Johnson Wax headquarters in Racine, Wisconsin, built in phases between 1939 and 1944 (figure 5.43).

The complex includes research laboratories, administrative offices, a large reception area, an executive suite, parking, a lecture theater, and support spaces. Mr. Johnson thought of his organization as an extended family under a benevolent patriarchy, and he wanted to reinvigorate his community by building in a struggling and ugly neighborhood. In response, Wright created an inward-looking building with few clear windows (the views would have been poor), though still well lighted. He asserted that the buildings were a "collective machine in which the social relationships were idealized in a clear diagram of institutional regulation and co-ordination."

The boldest feature of the building is the volume of the office atrium (figure 5.44) in the administration building, on the bottom of which is the open office plan for lower-level staff. Around the edges of the atrium rise tiers of offices for evermore senior managers, with the executives at the top. The atrium is still the lively focus of the facility.

The administration building's low mass is rounded and flowing; the 1944 research tower (hugely over budget) also has rounded edges in bands of brick, glass tubes, and the exposed edges of the concrete

Figure 5.44 Johnson Wax Office Atrium

floors. The main building was built with a new kind of structural "mushroom" column (figure 5.45); the research tower uses innovative alternating mezzanines cantilevered from a central concrete "tap root." Wright used new construction techniques to full advantage.

The interior colors are, as in many of Wright's designs, close cousins to those on the exterior, and reflect local materials and natural shades. It is wrong to call everything by Wright "Prairie Style," but it is true his palettes were of the earth.

The Johnson Wax building was the first to use piped in-floor heating. The furniture is as interesting as the building: Wright designed not only the desks and chairs, but the accessories, too. The experience of the building is intense, its inventiveness fitting the client's business mission.

Like Gropius, Wright created a school for architects, the Taliesin Fellowship, but unlike Gropius, Wright was prolific, evolving, and dependably contentious—a genius only the strongest leaders could work with as equals.

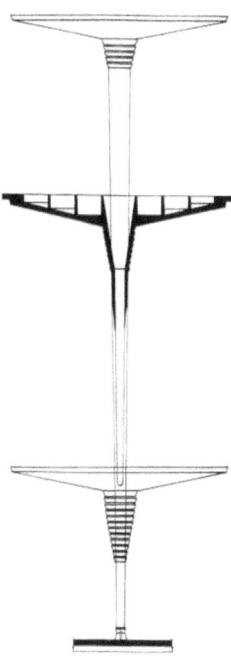

Figure 5.45 Wright "mushroom" column

Crown Hall (1956)

Figure 5.46 Crown Hall exterior

Ludwig Mies van der Rohe (1886–1969) took over the Bauhaus from Walter Gropius in 1930 before also escaping to America in 1937 to head the Illinois Institute of Technology's architecture school. IIT gave van der Rohe not only charge of the school, but the commission to design much of the campus, including Crown Hall (figure 5.46) in 1956.

"Mies" was the son of a master mason, apprenticed in furniture design and, like so many other young architects in Europe and America, took the "grand tour" of the classic buildings of Greece and Rome. (In 1910 he visited an exhibit in Germany of Frank Lloyd Wright's.) But Mies' own architecture ideals, like those of Gropius, stemmed largely from the social regeneration that new mass-production technologies promised. Mies thought buildings should use technology and materials as efficiently as possible; his designs are decidedly minimalist. It was Mies who said, "Less is more." Many see Miesian buildings as too stark; a later architect was to say, "Less is a bore." But Mies' thoughtful buildings let individual and social life flourish without distraction or waste.

Figure 5.47 Crown Hall interior

Crown Hall's clear-span interior (figure 5. 47) is made possible by the above-roof weight-bearing beams. Only low, freestanding walls divide its floor plan. There are lecture rooms and workshops in the garden level below. Sited to fit the grid of the IIT campus, it is surrounded by a flat lawn and paved areas to encourage students to gather informally as at the Bauhaus. Mies carefully chose native plants whose size fit the scale of the building.

The building is black and clear glass: some see the building as cold, while others feel Mies' intent to keep the building from distracting from the views of plants and human life. The photos show that the massing is extraordinarily simple, spare of everything unnecessary and illogical. The building has qualities like the ancient Roman and Greek structures Mies saw as a young man: symmetry, clear expression of structure, and simple rhythms of windows and columns. These straightforward proportions and elegant use of steel and glass are now so common that we need to remember that Mies was the inventor.

Crown Hall's interior colors and textures are based on the muted palette of dark gray and white-flecked terrazzo floors. The freestanding walls are in oak; the ceilings are white acoustic tiles—now another commonplace, but then quite new. This building highlights the bright reflected light within, an idea we saw at the Bauhaus and will see later in Louis Kahn's Kimbell Art Museum. Mies, like the other architects, was said to have a big ego, but his buildings reveal a kind of humility by taking the background to people and nature.

It was Mies who said, "God is in the details." There is decoration in Mies' buildings; he actually created covers to make the columns seem more genuine than the bare steel underneath. As in all the six buildings reviewed here, the architect designed furniture. Mies' "Barcelona chair" (figure 5.48) is everywhere and a clear extension of his architectural philosophy of using technology in design to give our lives focus.

Figure 5.48 Chair by Mies Van der Rohe

TWA Terminal (1962)

Eero Saarinen (1920–61) said, "I align myself humbly against Mies van der Rohe," and "The time is ripe for a new functional approach to a problem." Saarinen, a Finn and another son of an architect, purposely set out to be distinctive and memorable.

Figure 5.49 TWA Terminal

The TWA Terminal at New York's Idlewild (now JFK) Airport was finished in 1962 (figure 5.49). It was not the first time architects used concrete to shape flowing forms, but the size of the building and spectacular interior spaces were revolutionary (figure 5.50). Saarinen wanted to create a "form world" so passengers would have a consistent experience as they walked through the sequence of spaces, a kind of huge umbrella over the passenger areas. The modern visitor needs to imagine airports without today's intense crowds, security, and retail; air travel was then a tenth of what it is now and a luxury.

The TWA Terminal was sited near the entry to the airport, intending to create an incredible, futuristic first impression for the entire complex. The massing of the building was meant to convey the "drama, specialness, and excitement of travel." The shapes and floor plans create a sense of movement; the column shapes empha-

Figure 5.50 TWA information desk

size the soaring quality of the spaces, like the flaring mushroom columns of the Johnson Wax building. The wing shapes of the main roof are made of interlocking barrel vaults, as in a Romanesque cathedral.

Not only was the shape of the structure unique, so were the huge glass walls filling the large, odd-shaped wall openings. The size and curved outlines of the window walls seem unreal. The light, shadows, and sound reflecting on the white surfaces still create an atmosphere of another world. There is little freestanding furniture; the ticket and information counters follow the flowing shapes of the building. Saarinen took care that there were consistent shapes everywhere: in the signs, railings, and hardware. He knew the dramatic mood would collapse if any part of the architecture interrupted the story.

Kimbell Art Museum (1972)

Louis Kahn (1901–74) was a temperamental and absent-minded artist, and the design and construction of the Kimbell Art Museum in 1972 in Fort Worth, Texas was a saga of conflict (figure 5.51). But the result is sublime, and Kahn was right to fight for his ideas. One of three museums on a campus, the Kimbell's mission is to house an exquisite and varied private art collection.

Figure 5.51 Kimbell Art Museum exterior

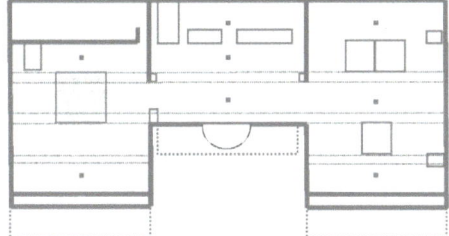

Figure 5.52 Kimbell Art Museum floor plan

The floor plan (figure 5.52) is symmetrical and formal, including galleries, a café, an auditorium, as well as the offices and studios every museum needs. The interior spaces are free flowing, with movable, partial-height partitions. Each gallery is 100 feet long and 20 feet wide and open to each other. The overall building is a fat U, with the entry centered on the inside. The interior courtyard, with large windows on all sides, offers a large bronze sculpture (Maillot's *L'Aire*) as a focus.

The arcades, reflecting pools, and orderly plantings anticipate the interior order. Kahn and the museum's leaders knew that the success of a museum depends hugely on the state of the mind of the visitor. The landscaping and exterior spaces, beautiful in themselves, create a gentle transition from the exterior to the interior. The sculpture garden—a simple lawn—is a sensible extension of the floor plan.

The building's structure is a bundle of the barrel-vaulted galleries, a simple idea brilliantly executed: each proportion is thoroughly considered. The consistent, classic interior volumes are dramatic. But it is the light (figure 5.53) that most impresses every visitor. The top ridge of each barrel vault has a slender longitudinal skylight, screened and reflected just under the ceiling to diffuse the intense Texas sun, perfect for the artwork.

There are no strong colors in the Kimbell. The walls are a creamy travertine marble and the floors are white oak like the interior walls of Crown Hall. These colors and textures enhance the warm quality of light and allow the paintings and sculptures to speak for themselves without distraction. The natural lighting is supplemented with spotlights to create what Kahn called a "well-lighted silence." There is mechanical ventilation

Figure 5.53 Kimbell Art Museum interior

at the Kimbell: it was a big challenge, but Kahn worked with the engineers to create spaces for ducts within the bases of the vaults.

The furniture is simple: strong, rectangular stone benches inside and out provide shapes that complement the building. The detailing is minimal, and the brushed stainless steel drinking fountains, door hardware, and handrails are as simple and elegant as the vaults. The Kimbell Art Museum, Kahn's last and favorite building is a flawless example of forms reflecting the practical and psychological needs of its visitors.

Trust an Artist

It should now be clear how important it is to select a talented architect; architectural skill is not a commodity. While not without strong passions, a skilled architect must be trusted to synthesize the nine elements of architecture into one meaningful and magnificent design. Chapter 6 deals with choosing the right architect.

Special Issues and Building Types

The ideas discussed so far apply to any type of architecture, but there are of course other issues about which more experienced or more interested newcomers may want to learn. For example, one fascinating topic is the architecture of different cultures of different periods: the architecture of ancient Rome is an exploration of politics, warfare, and social organization. The avant garde in architecture is also fascinating: young and old architects are creating forms and shaping cities—as in Berlin—that are of startling inventiveness and courage. An excellent springboard into the world of architecture is www.greatbuildings.com.

Specialty Buildings

The unique architectural issues for hospitals, schools, laboratories, stores, government buildings, military bases, museums, theaters, monuments (figure 5.54), and libraries are extensive. Peers and professional associations have lessons to share, but hiring an architect with relevant experience is the first step. That said, an architect with too narrow a specialization might not be as creative. This book aims to provide a framework for organizing ideas about the reader's own building.

Figure 5.54 Lincoln Memorial

Sustainability

The first concern of *sustainability* in architecture is for energy use: a "green" building uses as little energy as possible to build and operate. Recycling and reusing materials save energy in the production of steel, wood, concrete, and cable, but good planning is also conserving: even a small unnecessary renovation wastes more energy and produces more trash than can be saved in a year's effort to recycle copy paper. An environmentally conscious leader, who might represent environmentally conscious shareholders, should ask the architect for a presentation on green building initiatives. He or she should learn at least a little about LEED (Leadership in Energy and Environmental Design) certification from the U.S. Green Building Council (www.usgbc.com).

Industrial Engineering

Determining the complex practical functionality of a manufacturing plant or distribution center is the job of an industrial engineer (as consultant to the architect). Science can be applied to quantify and optimize workflows and storage density and to design

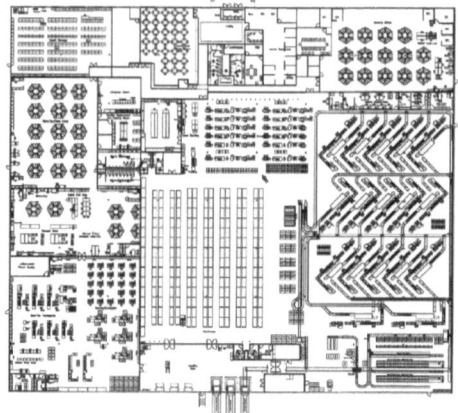

Figure 5.55 Factory floor plan

conveyors and other material handling equipment (figure 5.55). The relationships among computerization, equipment, and space use can be complex. While the need for industrial engineering is obvious for a large manufacturer, many smaller plants and warehouses fail because the leader did not get a professional to calculate the right aisle widths, conveyor pathways, and equipment placement. Many industrial facilities are crippled by being one foot too narrow or one foot too low.

Historic Preservation

Some leaders will face the choice of whether to renovate a very old building. Many old buildings are simply that—old—but it can be surprising how attached a community can be to old, but ugly schools, churches, and town halls. Every leader should become acquainted with the community's architectural history. Some buildings are of genuine architectural importance and protected by law; one hopes to find an architectural treasure. It can be a challenge to preserve the charm of an old building while adapting its spaces and systems to make it work for your purposes. Historic preservation is a well-established architectural specialty.

New Urbanism and Sprawl

New Urbanists are concerned about the shape, quality, and character of cities, their greenspace, traffic, housing, and architecture. Communities are passing "smart growth" laws requiring land use plans that restrict geographic spread. Anti-sprawl sentiment is gaining political force because of the wasteful consumption of farmland for houses that are simply too large. In several places in America, towns and neighborhoods are being designed and built as a whole, including Seaside, Florida and Middleton Hills in Wisconsin (the brainchild of a Wright disciple). Leaders face the ethical decisions of whether their building enriches or dilutes its community. At the least, the leader should study the community's land use and transportation plans. The Congress for New Urbanism provides facts and philosophies (www.cnu.org).

Religious Architecture

While the reader may not be commissioning a church, the study of religious architecture is an excellent way to learn about buildings with spirit. This book began with the example of how a church has both practical and psychological functions. The breadth of religious architecture is wide, from Norwegian wooden stave churches to contemporary synagogues to delicately tiled mosques to Buddhist temples carved into caves. Their history is an exploration of humility and power, transition and tolerance, and control and freedom of expression—of every century in every country. The Hagia Sophia (figure 5.56) was built in 532 A.D. in Istanbul by the Emperor Justinian as a Christian church but is now a mosque. The 21st century is beginning with noteworthy churches by Renzo Piano and Richard Meier.

Figure 5.56 Hagia Sophia, Istanbul

Schools and Styles

The 20th century sparked hugely diverse architectural styles, some of which we discussed earlier in this chapter. Even summarizing the popular styles of the past 100 years would take as many pages, so we will content ourselves with this partial list in roughly chronological order: Neoclassical, Modern, Arts and Crafts, International, Nouveau, Prairie, Deco, Moderne, Postmodern, and Deconstructivism, among others. There are also the traditional styles—Greek Revival, Victorian, Beaux Arts, Colonial, Federal, Mission—and the local styles of Nantucket, New Orleans, Philadelphia, Florida's Palm Coast, and on and on. And there are individualistic buildings that fit no school—some wonderful, some terrible.

6 · Executive Team and Tasks

Organize to Delegate

A large project will involve dozens of professionals in addition to the architect's specialists and the builder's subcontractors. It is beyond this book's scope to describe them all, but a typical project team is listed below in alphabetical order. The time line (figure 6.1, next page) provides a general idea of the sequence of activities.

- Accountants
- Appraisers
- Attorneys
- Bankers
- Brokers
- Developers
- Equipment suppliers
- Facility consultants
- Financial advisors
- Fundraising experts
- Furniture dealers
- Insurance agents
- Investment bankers
- IT experts
- Movers
- Project managers
- PR advisors
- Regulators
- Soils specialists
- Surveyors
- Telephony providers

Delegating Creativity

After creating the project plan and after all the hard work of articulating the building's location, finances, and many practical and psychological functions, the leader must turn to the architect to create the design. *Creativity* means blending the nine elements of architecture into a single form that meets all the leader's practical and psychological requirements. A good architect knows that creativity can be fostered within a practice that encourages talented, trained, and experienced people to do their best. A good architect also knows that an act of creativity can be conjured up with clear objectives, clear information, and gentle pressure.

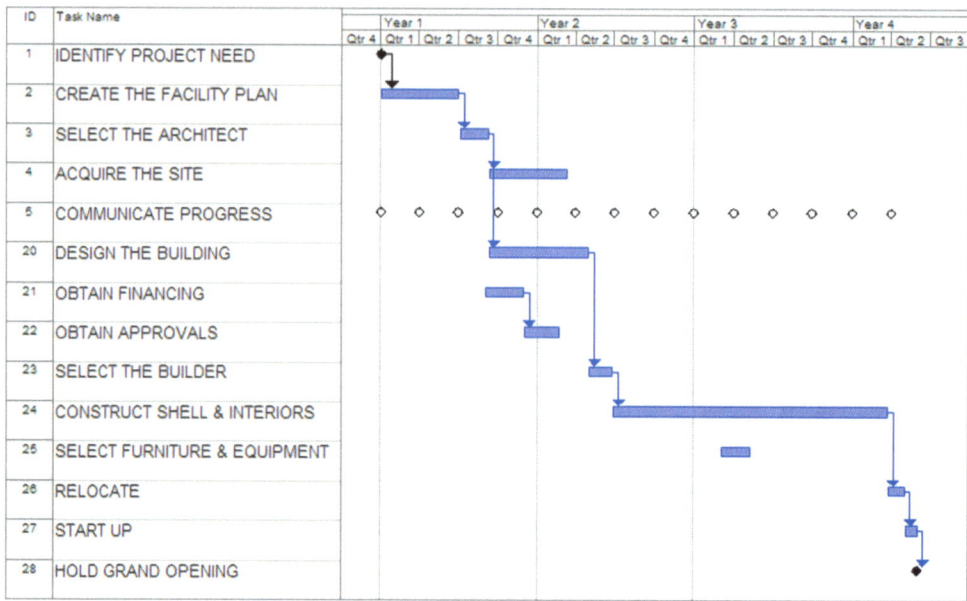

Figure 6.1 Project management time line (Gantt chart)

Hiring the Architect

Every leader knows how to hire professionals in a professional way and will ask about the candidates' specialties and credentials and will study their personalities. What may be new is having to gauge artistic talent: that judgment is based on the variety, quality, and style of the architect's portfolio. Past clients should speak of them and their buildings with admiration.

One way to select an architect is through a contest, but a contest cannot produce a thoughtful design: it does not give the contestants enough time to learn all the leader must accomplish, nor does it allow the development of a close relationship between client and architect.

Styles

Everyone has his or her own style. A style emerges from the thousands of conscious and subconscious decisions we make when creating something complex like a building. Style is how we manifest our personalities in what we create.

What happens when we hire someone else to express *our* needs and dreams? Naturally, we like to know their style is similar to, or at least in tune with, our own. Should a leader hire an architect because he or she likes their style? Or should the leader search for an architect who has the ability to express each client's unique style?

Interview Questions

In a perfect interview, the candidate anticipates every question and asks good questions in return. But here are a few questions that probe for an architect's most important qualifications:

- ❏ Are their buildings unique to each client, or does their work only express themselves?
- ❏ Are they aware how their buildings have helped their clients succeed?
- ❏ Have their clients found pleasant surprises in their buildings?
- ❏ How do they set a realistic budget? A realistic schedule?
- ❏ What creative things have they done to meet tight budgets and schedules?
- ❏ How do they conjure creativity when it is needed?
- ❏ How do they balance artistry with professional project management?
- ❏ How do they educate their clients about architecture?
- ❏ Do they explain why having enough time is important?

Every leader should consider hiring an architect who will support them through their entire career. It is common to choose attorneys, accountants, and management consultants with this end in mind.

Unveilings

Once the architect is hired, he or she must be given time to complete the project plan and to discuss and refine the narrative of all the practical and psychological functions. This takes several months.

Surprising Alternatives

After the planning and analysis, the architect must then produce three or four viable conceptual designs, so the leader can be confident the architect has considered all the possibilities. While the leader will have visions of the building, they will never compare to the architect's. Only part of this evaluation can be made rationally: intuition is the seat of the best decisions. Some architects are better than others at explaining what they have created, but an inarticulate architect may be the best designer.

Elegant Solutions

A test of a good design is whether it fulfills several functions with one feature: a glass door provides entry and light, but a door with an operable window provides entry, light, air circulation, *and* privacy. A well-designed courtyard gives shelter and shade as well as helpful edges and thoughtful views. A building should be full of these elegant efficiencies.

Final Design Decision

To meet his or her responsibilities in architecture, the leader must depend on intuition for hundreds of decisions reflecting the organization's vision and values. This is how a building comes to reflect the leader's style and not that of the architect. We began with all the reasons building is an opportunity for leadership; it follows that good decisions cannot be made by a committee.

The leader *must* be confident that the conceptual design serves *all* the practical and psychological functions as well as the objectives of the business case (Chapter 2). A committee or board might offer an opinion or challenge, but the risks and rewards are the leader's.

Picture It

The leader who has come to the point of approving a building design should imagine taking a customer, employee, board member, or donor on a personal tour. If the leader does not feel in their gut that the design is the best it can be, he or she should revisit each objective and element discussed in Chapter 5 until they can articulate the problem—and then direct the architect to revise the drawings accordingly. It is time to build only when the design feels absolutely right.

The Sequence of Documents

Our first purpose is to teach a leader to work with their architect to create a good design; it is not our purpose to discuss all the ins and outs of engineering and construction. That said, a good leader must understand the tasks he or she delegates. This section summarizes how a design becomes a building.

Programming

Programming, the analysis of space needs, was done as part of the project plan and business case. During this phase of the design, the architect establishes a team, sets deadlines, establishes communications, and confirms all the assumptions in the project plan. It is wise to revisit these assumptions when weighing the conceptual designs.

Schematic Design

Schematic design documents are a simple set of drawings: a site plan, floor plans, elevations (side views), and sometimes cross-sections or interior elevations. These drawings are essential to setting the budget. The architect may also produce color renderings, detailed models, and perspective drawings. At some point after the creation and refinement of the schematic design, the leader should shout, "That's it!" The schematics confirm whether the best synthesis of all the elements has really happened.

Design Development

The schematics evolve into the *design development drawings,* which include all the critical dimensions, material selections, schedules (tables) of each door and room finish, preliminary engineering drawings, landscaping plans, and an outline specification book. The design development documents include more detailed drawings about cabinetry and construction details. A builder or estimator can use this enhanced information to update the budget and schedule.

At this point, many leaders see that the executive decisions have been made and they can comfortably delegate the project's implementation. The architect, too, may delegate this production work to other staff.

Construction Documents

Construction documents are the rolls of detailed drawings and the thick specification book that fully define not only what to build but how to build it to the prescribed level of quality. If the drawings and details are neat and clear, if not in fact beautifully done, the builders are reminded daily how much others care about their crafts. Few leaders read these documents closely, but should have a representative who does. These documents form the traditional bid set and are eventually found in every contractor's trailer on the job site.

Contract Administration

The architect's responsibilities continue through construction, observing the work and solving the inevitable problems of transforming two-dimensional drawings into three-dimensional reality. The architect and engineers check the subcontractors' *shop drawings* (descriptions of the smallest details of construction), prepare job meeting notes, certify percents of work complete in the contractor's applications for payments, and issue certificates of substantial and final completion. One of their last tasks is to write a *punchlist*, a room-by-room list of all the little things that the builder must correct or complete to be finally finished and fully paid. A punchlist might note a cracked switch plate, an unlabelled electrical panel, or a scratched cabinet.

An architect often has a specialist conducting the contract administration: a good contract administrator is a different personality type than a designer. The leader should attend most of the weekly or biweekly job meetings and visit the site to show every tradesperson he or she cares about the job being done.

The Builder

Different Roles for a Builder

A *general contractor* is the builder's traditional role: he or she holds each subcontract (earthwork, structural steel, carpentry, and so forth) and manages the entire job. A *construction manager* is similar, though the owner of the building holds the subcontracts, a subtle advantage in risk management generally unimportant to small projects. A *design-builder* actually has the architect working for them, which lets the builder control the design and, therefore, the budget.

Money and time and quality are everything in construction, and a builder's scheduling ability is a test of that skill. The owner should ask every week, Are we on budget? Are we on time? Have we had to compromise quality? Tough persistence on questions of cost and schedule is essential because the stakes are high and candor can weaken.

Builder Selection

Builders were traditionally selected from bids based on a detailed analysis (*take-off*) of all the construction documents. The problems with this approach are that the leader waits a long time to be certain of the project's cost and is left with little time to adjust. A popular solution is to select the builder soon after the architect is selected, using the builders' credentials and percentage mark-ups as the basis of competition for the job. In this way, the leader and architect can tap the builder's estimating and construction knowledge to refine the design while in process. This increases certainty in the cost and schedule (for example, the builder may know that the proposed mechanical equipment is hard to get) and decreases the disruption and delays of changes during construction.

Here are some questions for interviewing potential builders:
- ❑ How do you define quality?
- ❑ What is your quality assurance program?
- ❑ How do you ensure job safety?
- ❑ How do you keep morale high?
- ❑ What makes an architect excellent?
- ❑ How can you prove your thoroughness?

Changes and Disagreements

Most leaders are expert project managers. They will know to create a strong team, establish controls, communicate objectives, and make decisions promptly. It is impossible, however, to write construction documents that capture all the leader's ideas and anticipate every contingency. The drawings and even the first phases of construction invariably spark new ideas important to the leader. Changes and problems are of course inevitable.

There is much at stake, but resolving disputes about money, time, and responsibility are familiar territory to an experienced leader. Objectivity, budget contingencies, prompt action, and tight contracts keep the project moving toward success, though the most important way to reduce conflict is to select an architect and a builder who are top-notch.

7 • Grand Opening

Having a building designed and built is a long journey, but the overarching goal is a building that fulfills the promise of the business case and is so thoughtfully done it needs no renovation for many years.

A new building is a chance to host community gatherings, issue press releases, and give personal tours to customers, board members, and investors. The grand opening is certainly worth celebrating, but it is only one milestone.

Figure 7.1 Amish barn raising

Every leader must tell and retell their organization's story with enthusiasm and conviction. At the entry, the leader might pause to relate the organization's history and point to service or product displays. Walking past the work areas, through the corridors, and stopping where people socialize, the leader can share their vision of the organization's culture, challenges, and plans. The tour should end, like any story, with a brave promise of continued success.

Acknowledgments

Architects, educators, and gentlemen, Charles Davis of Davis Associates, David Kuffner of OWP/P, and Joe Valerio of Valerio Dewalt Train were more than generous with their time, rich experience, and patience. My brothers Robert and Rick gave me the advice and wisdom I have always depended on, and Mary Kay Van Mell's warm words of encouragement were also and always deeply appreciated. There were many other helpful readers: Roger Axtell, Vanessa Balchen, Gary Broersma, John Devereux, Barb Irvin and Jay Knight included. I hope this book reflects a small part of my parents' intellect, curiosity, and skill with words. Much of the credit for this book is clearly elsewhere; the mistakes are mine.

BIBLIOGRAPHY

Alexander, Christopher, et al. 1977. *A Pattern Language: Towns, Buildings, Construction*, Oxford University Press.

Brownlee, David B. and DeLong, David G. 1991. *Louis Kahn: In the Realm of Architecture*. Rizzoli.

Carter, Peter. 1974. *Mies van der Rohe at Work.* Praeger Publication.

www.cnu.org Congress for New Urbanism

Conway, Hazel and Roenisch, Rowan. 1994. *Understanding Architecture.* Routledge.

Cruickshank, Dan, ed. 2000. *Architecture: The Critics Choice.* Watson-Guptill Publications.

Curtis, William J. R. 1996. *Modern Architecture since 1900.* 3rd edition. Phaidon.

www.esri.com

www.greatbuildings.com

Grillo, Paul Jacques. 1960. *Form, Function and Design.* Dover Publications.

Gropius, Walter. 1965. *The New Architecture and the Bauhaus.* MIT Press.

Kamin, Blair. 2001. *Why Architecture Matters.* University of Chicago Press.

Komendant, August. 1975. *18 Years with Architect Louis Kahn.* Alornay.

Kostof, Spiro. 1985. *A History of Architecture.* Oxford University Press.

Monmonier, Mark, 1996. *How to Lie With Maps.* University of Chicago Press.

Rasmussen, Steen Eiler. 1959. *Experiencing Architecture.* MIT Press.

Ruskin, John. (1853) 1989. *The Seven Lamps of Architecture.* General Publishing.

Saarinen, Aline B., ed. 1962. *Eero Saarinen on His Work.* Yale University Press.

Stein, Hatch, Stanton, and Peterson. 1997. *Monticello.* Thomas Jefferson Memorial Foundation, Inc.

Sullivan, Louis H. 1979. *Kindergarten Chats.* Dover Publications.

Wright, Frank Lloyd. (1901) 1943. *Frank Lloyd Wright an Autobiography.* Barnes and Noble.

www.usgbc.com U.S. Green Building Council

www.vanmell.com Van Mell Associates

Visser, Kristin. 1992. *Frank Lloyd Wright and the Prairie School in Wisconsin.* Prairie Oak Press.

Wolfe, Tom. 1981. *From Bauhaus to Our House.* Farrar Straus Giroux.

IMAGE CREDITS

Figure 1.1	The Pentagon: Space Imaging, www.spaceimaging.com
Figure 1.2	Hitler and building model, 1937: Postcard, photographer unknown.
Figure 1.3	Hitler's office, Nazi postcard: Postcard image, photographer unknown.
Figure 2.1	Project planning logic: Van Mell Associates
Figure 2.2	ROI Worksheet: Van Mell Associates
Figure 2.3	Project scorecard: Van Mell Associations
Figure 2.4	Goodman Community Center Map: Van Mell Associates
Figure 2.5	Space use allocation: Van Mell Associates
Figure 2.6	Block plan: Van Mell Associates
Figure 3.1	ZIP code map: Van Mell Associates
Figure 3.2	Scatter map: Van Mell Associates
Figure 3.3	Multi-layout map: Van Mell Associates
Figure 3.4	Aerial view of Lincoln and Washington monumnets. Courtesy of the U.S. Geologic Survey
Figure 3.5	Site selection matrix: Van Mell Associates
Figure 3.6	Scatter map: Van Mell Associates
Figure 3.7	Store location analysis: Current Analysis West
Figure 3.8	Wisconsin bank branch analysis: Van Mell Associates
Figure 3.9	K-12 school district analysis: Applied Population Lab
Figure 3.10	Manufacturer/distributor transport web: Van Mell Associates
Figure 3.11	Service firm client access: Van Mell Associates
Figure 3.12	Community center service area: Van Mell Associates
Figure 3.13	A well-designed map: Van Mell Associates
Figure 3.14	Layer 1 of 4: Demographics base map: Van Mell Associates
Figure 3.15	Layer 2 of 4: Customer scatter map: Van Mell Associates
Figure 3.16	Layer 3 of 4: Circles to add focus: Van Mell Associates
Figure 3.17	Layer 4 of 4: Drive time and market shift: Van Mell Associates
Figure 4.1	Project budget: Van Mell Associates
Figure 4.2	ROI worksheet: Van Mell Associates
Figure 4.3	Leasing versus owning: Van Mell Associates
Figure 4.4	Facility scorecard: Van Mell Associates
Figure 5.1	Block plan: Van Mell Associates
Figure 5.2	Reception desk concept sketch: Linville Architects
Figure 5.3	Monticello floor plan: Monticello / Thomas Jefferson Foundation, Inc.
Figure 5.4	Church entry: istockphoto.com
Figure 5.5	Commerzbank cafeteria in Frankfurt: Nigel Young / Foster and Partners
Figure 5.6	Rockefeller Plaza: Vanessa Balchen
Figure 5.7	Commerzbank garden in Frankfurt: Nigel Young / Foster and Partners
Figure 5.8	Machu Picchu in Peru: Jennifer Gregan-Paxton
Figure 5.9	Monticello set in nature: Matt Kozlowski. See Note 1.
Figure 5.10	Guggenheim Museum in Bilbao: Myk Reeve. See Note 1.

Figure 5.11   The Golden Section proportions: Jon Brouchoud, Crescendo Design
Figure 5.12   Le Modular: Jon Brouchoud, Crescendo Design
Figure 5.13   Guggenheim asymmetrical entry: Alessandra. See Note 2.
Figure 5.14   Generic architecture: Vanessa Balchen
Figure 5.15   3COM campus in Illinois: Kelly Martin. See Note 1.
Figure 5.16   Osaka Castle: Cesare Polenghi
Figure 5.17   Fallingwater: Michael Ryan / GreatBuildings.com
Figure 5.18   Service garage: Potter Lawson
Figure 5.19   John Hancock building, Chicago: istockphoto.com
Figure 5.20   White architecture (Getty Museum): istockphoto.com
Figure 5.21   Tower of Pisa: Peter Bagnall
Figure 5.22   Farnsworth House: Peter G. Palumbo / Friends of the Farnsworth House
Figure 5.23   Grand Central Station: Corbis
Figure 5.24   Rose Center at night: Carol Bracewell, Flying Pig Productions
Figure 5.25   Architectural elevation drawing: OWP/P
Figure 5.26   Wayfinding colors and textures: OWP/P
Figure 5.27   Monticello colors: Robert C. Lautman / Thomas Jefferson Foundation, Inc.
Figure 5.28   Lighting for good work: Jon Brouchoud, Crescendo Design
Figure 5.29   Retail lighting types: Larry Bolch
Figure 5.30   Wisconsin State Capitol: Dave Parker. See Note 1.
Figure 5.31   Chair by Walter Gropius: Knoll, Inc.
Figure 5.32   Chair by Mies van der Rohe: Knoll, Inc.
Figure 5.33   FDR in the Oval Office, 1935: Courtesy of the FDR Library Digital Archives
Figure 5.34   Notre Dame: istockphotos.com
Figure 5.35   *American Gothic* (detail), Grant Wood: Corbis
Figure 5.36   Monticello approach: Matt Kozlowski. See Note 1.
Figure 5.37   Monticello floor plan: Monticello / Thomas Jefferson Foundation, Inc.
Figure 5.38   Monticello dining room fireplace:
               Monticello / Thomas Jefferson Foundation, Inc.
Figure 5.39   Postcard of the Bauhaus Building in Dessau, Germany, 1927: Collection of Harald Wetzel
Figure 5.40   Bauhaus floor plan: Jon Brouchoud, Crescendo Design
Figure 5.41   Bauhaus Building auditorium 1926/27: Collection of Harald Wetzel
Figure 5.42   Chair by Walter Gropius: Knoll, Inc.
Figure 5.43   Johnson Wax Research Tower: From public domain.
Figure 5.44   Johnson Wax Office Atrium: From public domain.
Figure 5.45   Wright "mushroom" column: Dr. Ted Kesik, P.Eng.
Figure 5.46   Crown Hall exterior: Jeremy Atherton. See Note 2.
Figure 5.47   Crown Hall interior: Bob Thall
Figure 5.48   Chair by Mies Van der Rohe: Knoll, Inc.
Figure 5.49   TWA Terminal: Ron Saari
Figure 5.50   TWA information desk: Michael Weitnauer / GreatBuildings.com
Figure 5.51   Kimbell Art Museum exterior: Michael Bodycomb photographer
               © Kimbell Art Museum 2005
Figure 5.52   Kimbell Art Museum floor plan: Derrick Van Mell
Figure 5.53   Kimbell Art Museum interior: Jmabel. See Note 1.
Figure 5.54   Lincoln Memorial: istockphotos.com
Figure 5.55   Factory floor plan: Bodi Engineering
Figure 5.56   Hagia Sophia, Istanbul: istockphotos.com
Figure 6.1   Project management time line: Van Mell Associates
Figure 7.1   Amish barn raising: Ian Adams

Note 1: Image available under GNU Free Documentation License.
Note 2: Image available under Creative Commons Attribution Share Alike 2.0

ABOUT THE AUTHOR

Derrick Van Mell is an expert in how business and buildings connect. He founded Van Mell Associates in 1991 with the mission of helping his clients decide how buildings can best support their strategic plans. He was worked on projects in healthcare, research, manufacturing, distribution, and services, as well as for non-profit organizations of all kinds. He recognizes that success begins with efficiency and high return on investment and ends with a building that inspires everyone.

Mr. Van Mell has a BA in Economics, an MBA in finance, and an MA in English. He has had the privilege of working with creative, accomplished, and thoughtful architects in master planning and programming assignments for many clients. He is also the author of *Question-Based Planning: Planning without Mission, Vision, Strategy, Tactics, or Objectives*.

Mr. Van Mell has been published widely, spoken internationally, and been a Guest Lecturer at the University of Wisconsin. A Chicago native, he now lives in Madison, Wisconsin. More about Mr. Van Mell and his firm can be found at www.vanmell.com. He can be reached at (608) 260-9300 or derrick@vanmell.com.